Published by Franz Gutwenger

East Stroudsburg - Pennsylvania

ISBN: 979-8-9940908-0-0

First Edition

This book is a work of nonfiction. While the author has made every effort to ensure the accuracy of the information contained herein, the content is provided for educational purposes only and does not constitute financial, legal, or investment advice. Trading involves risk, and readers are encouraged to conduct their own due diligence and consult with a qualified professional before making trading decisions. The author and publisher assume no responsibility for any losses or damages arising from the use of this material.

Printed in the United States of America.

i

"The Ultimate Traders Mindset" is designed to be more than something you read once and place on a shelf. It's a guide you can keep within reach on your desk, in your workspace, wherever you make decisions. Its purpose is to continually reinforce the mindset principles that shape clarity, resilience, and disciplined action. By returning to it daily, even in small doses, you strengthen the foundation that supports both consistent performance and long-term growth.

In today's era of rapidly evolving AI, leveraging the most advanced tools is essential to maintain a competitive edge and maximize our potential.

With self-paced learning, you're free to take in the concepts at your own speed - slowly and deeply, or in quick bursts when inspiration strikes. The flexibility to revisit key chapters means you can reinforce what matters most, exactly when you need it.

Whether you turn to this book as a cost-effective way to access the material or as a powerful primer before attending a live workshop, it is designed to deepen your understanding and make the overall experience even more impactful.

Utilizing Neuro Linguistic Programming (NLP), Gestalt and Generative Coaching as base for your innovation!

Acknowledgements

Let me express my gratitude to all the thought leaders, explorers, researchers, and creative minds who have devoted years of their lives to unraveling the mysteries of human thinking, behavior, and being. Their work has provided the foundational building blocks of the knowledge we draw upon today. In doing so, they have expanded our sensory awareness and opened pathways for us to learn, experience, and integrate new ways of perceiving the world.

Using this book as your manual will offer you insights that illuminate blind spots outside your current awareness and introduce you to techniques and methodologies that support meaningful change and transformation.

For many years, I have immersed myself in the field of humanistic psychology, actively participated in workshops and retreats. Along the way, I had the good fortune to meet and learn from inspiring thought leaders and pioneers of emerging disciplines. Each of them contributed to expanding my understanding of the human condition - its self-imposed limitations, its potential, and the pathways toward fuller self-expression and contentment.

My special thanks to Dr. Wolf Buentig – founder of ZIST, Lynne Conwell - Founder and President of "The American Center for Advance Studies in NLP & EHF", Richard Bandler, Leslie Cameron Bandler, Michael Lebeau, Robert Dilts and others who advanced the development of NLP – Neurolinguistic Programming.

While this book has a particular focus on trading, the underlying principles apply to all humans in general and can be used widely in any domain where clarity, emotional regulation, decision-making, and self-leadership are essential. Whether you are navigating relationships, building a business, leading a team, or pursuing personal growth, the same psychological foundations remain relevant and transformative.

"The Ultimate Traders Mindset"

Confidence – Competence – Consistency

When we in pursuit of mastery whether in trading, coaching, leadership, or personal development - three forces form a self-reinforcing loop: confidence, competence, and consistency. Each element feeds the others, shaping not only performance but identity. When understood and intentionally cultivated, this triangle becomes a powerful framework for sustainable growth and emotional resilience.

Confidence: The Spark of Initiative

Confidence is the quiet assurance that comes from knowing and trusting yourself. It is a felt sense of possibility, a belief that one's actions can lead to meaningful outcomes. It's the emotional fuel that allows us to take risks, speak up, and engage with uncertainty. But confidence without substance is brittle. It thrives when grounded in competence and is reinforced by consistency. To quote Henry Ford I "Whether you believe you can or you can't you are always right". This is where confidence ties right into our belief systems.

Competence: The Substance Beneath the Surface

Competence is the actual skill, knowledge, or capacity to perform. It's what makes confidence credible. When we know what we're doing - when we've trained, studied, practiced, and refined - confidence becomes a natural byproduct. Competence also tempers overconfidence.

It cultivates humility through the lessons of feedback, mistakes, and continual refinement. Importantly, competence is not static; it evolves through consistent effort.

Consistency: Is the bridge that turns possibility into performance.

It is the silent force that transforms competence into confidence. It's the daily practice, the repeated exposure, the disciplined execution that builds trust - not just with others, but within us. Consistency creates evidence. It turns "I think I can" into "I know I can." Without consistency, competence remains dormant, and confidence fades under pressure.

The skills we acquire in life are shaped by cognitive modeling; we mirror behaviors, internalizing strategies and adapting them to our own style. We utilize feedback loops internally - self-reflective mechanisms that help us interpret experience and refine our sense of self, and externally - other people's input, measurable outcomes, or environmental responses. This process allow us to refine our approach and recalibrate. They act as process guides by continuously informing and adjusting our actions based on desired results. Creating a dynamic cycle of observation, reflection, and adaptation helping us stay aligned with goals, improve performance, and evolve with changing conditions. When "Chunking up or down" we either break complex tasks into manageable chunks, or we move from specific details to broader categories or purposes. Over time, we recognize patterns and automate sequences - like rehearsing a sequence until your body knows it better than your mind. But one of the most powerful ways is intentional purposeful practice, fine-tuning and adjusting to circumstances. This is the kind of learning we will be engaging in this book.

When I turned sixty, I decided I wanted to ski race. While in my teens I participated in a few races. The word "participated" fully reflects my level of commitment at that time. Since this was a portion of my life I really never lived, there was still a silent yearning to do this. Suddenly, recreational skiing was no longer enough. Every time I got on the mountain, I skied with purpose and intention, practicing technique as close to perfection as I could manage. And I loved every moment of it.

"Passion is forged on the anvil of desire"

What do you desire? Let's start with a reframing exercise.

To enhance your development as a trader and taking trading to different level what are you willing to do? Consider trading as means for personal evolution and the financial markets not just as a place to make money, but as a mirror that reflects your mindset, habits, fears, and strengths. Every trade becomes a feedback loop for self-awareness - exposing impatience, ego, discipline, adaptability, the level of confidence and emotional control.

In this frame, success is less about beating the market and

more about becoming the kind of person who can consistently make sound decisions under uncertainty. Drawdowns test your resilience, volatility challenges your emotional regulation, and profits test your humility. Over time, the same skills that make you a better trader- self-discipline, strategic thinking, flexibility, patience - also transform how you navigate your life.

When perceiving trading this way, trading isn't just a financial pursuit; it's a long-term practice of growth where the charts are your meditation mat, the trades are your experiments, and your evolving self is the real return on investment.

Are you willing to be open to new experiences and to explore some unknown territory?

Creating a mindset of curiosity and flexibility makes unexpected results possible that lead to real advancements.

Introduction and Overview

The value of understanding and applying NLP and Gestalt methods in trading lies in their ability to reveal the hidden structures behind thought, perception, and behavior. Both disciplines invite us to become aware of the unconscious patterns shaping the way we interpret events and make decisions, and to gain choice where previously there was only automaticity. In trading, where outcomes are uncertain and **emotional intensity can distort judgment**, the precision of NLP offers tools to recognize limiting beliefs, distorted cause-effect patterns, or unhelpful internal dialogues. Gestalt methods, with their emphasis on present-moment awareness and integration of fragmented parts of the self, allow traders to notice the tensions, projections, and unfinished experiences that might surface under pressure, thereby preventing these from unconsciously steering their actions. The real strength emerges when both approaches are combined: NLP provides the structure to reframe perceptions, shift meta-programs, and build more resourceful strategies, while Gestalt adds depth by fostering embodied awareness, emotional integration, and the capacity to hold paradox rather than rush to premature closure. The capacity to hold paradox is the ability to tolerate and engage with conflicting ideas, emotions, or realities without forcing an immediate resolution. Instead of rushing to simplify or choose one side, it allows for deeper understanding, creative problem solving, and more nuanced decision making. Beyond trading, these methods enrich everyday life by enhancing and understanding how we and others communicate, sharpening awareness of how we construct reality, and fostering a more authentic connection with ourselves and others. They illuminate how values, beliefs, and perceptions can either constrain or empower, and provide ways to expand choice so that we are less bound by automatic responses and more guided by conscious alignment. In relationships, this might mean listening not just to the words spoken but also to the unspoken patterns of contact and withdrawal; in leadership, it might mean recognizing how one's inner state colors the field of interaction; in personal growth, it might mean realizing that what felt like an external obstacle was in fact a projection of an unacknowledged part of oneself. The enduring value of NLP and Gestalt lies in their practical synthesis of awareness and change: the understanding that real transformation isn't achieved through techniques alone, but through learning to perceive with greater clarity, to inhabit your own experience with deeper presence, and to make choices with a level of consciousness that reshapes who you are becoming.

Why Trading Is 80% Mindset

Most traders arrive at the financial markets believing the secret to success lies in finding the perfect strategy, the flawless indicator, or the hidden market pattern that others can't see. They pour hours into back testing systems, refining entry and exit signals, and optimizing stop-loss levels. Yet, despite all that technical effort, the same story plays out:

They hesitate when it's time to take a trade.

They cut winners too soon.

They hold onto losers, hoping they'll turn around.

They revenge-trade after a loss, breaking every rule they swore to follow.

If you ever experienced these cycles, then this sounds all very familiar and you already know the truth: trading is not just about the markets but equally important is your mindset navigating them.

With this book you will be familiarized with the hidden - out of your awareness - mental patterns determining your experience, behavior, actions and the outcome you are creating. In NLP they are called Meta Programs. Meta Programs are unconscious mental strategies that determine how we process information. They act as filters, influencing attention, motivation, decision making, and communication. Think of them as the "software" running in the background of the mind, guiding behavior without us realizing it. Adjust one Meta Program, and you are able to reach different outcomes.

The financial markets are the world's greatest mirror. They reflect your patience, your discipline, your resilience and your fears, doubts, and impulsive urges. Every trade is a conversation between your strategy and your psychology. And in that conversation, psychology wins far more often than most traders want to admit.

This book is about taking control of these internal processes.

In short: Neuro-Linguistic Programming (NLP) is the art and science of understanding how we structure our thoughts, emotions, and behaviors - and how to rewire them for optimal performance. It has been used for decades to accelerate learning, build confidence, overcome fears, and create unshakable mental states in high-pressure fields such as sports, public speaking, and negotiation.

Now, we bring it into the world of trading.

In the following chapters, you'll discover how to:

Identify and break the mental patterns sabotaging your trading results.

Use language - both spoken and internal - to shift your emotional state instantly.

Anchor peak performance states before and during market hours.

Reframe losses so they become fuel for progress rather than scars on your confidence.

Build a trading identity aligned with your values and long-term goals.

Whether you're a beginner still building your first strategy or a seasoned trader who's hit a plateau, the tools in this book will help you close the gap between knowing what to do and actually doing it consistently, under pressure, and without self-sabotage.

The market will always be uncertain. The next candle, the next move, the next trend - these are outside your control.

But you can master the trader making the decisions.

And when you do, you stop playing the market's game and start playing your own.

"Welcome to the journey of becoming a mindful, self-aware trader"

The Ultimate Trader's Mindset - Complete NLP Toolkit

Part I - How we process information and create experiences

Experience does not simply happen to us - it's what we make of what happens. Every moment we are flooded with signals: sights, sounds, sensations, words, gestures. But these raw inputs don't become experience by itself until they pass through the intricate architecture of our inner world. We are not passive receivers; **we are architects of meaning**. As a friend of mine uses to say: "We are meaning-making machines"

Internally, information is never neutral. It enters through the senses, but is immediately filtered by memory, emotion, expectation, and identity. A raised eyebrow might register as curiosity to one person, criticism to another. A market dip might feel like opportunity to a seasoned trader, threat to a novice. The same external event becomes a thousand different internal realities, shaped by the lens through which it's seen.

This lens is built from layers. First, there's the somatic layer - the body's immediate response. Tightness in the chest, warmth in the belly, a sudden jolt of adrenaline. These sensations are fast, primal, and often unconscious. They signal safety or danger before thought arrives. Then comes the emotional layer: the feelings that colors perception. Joy, anxiety, fear, frustration, shame, sadness, longing - these emotions act as filters, amplifying or distorting what we notice. However confidence is changing the game.

Next is the cognitive layer, where interpretation begins. Here, the mind searches for patterns, matches the moment to memory, and begins to narrate. "This reminds me of…" "This always happens when…" "I knew this would go wrong…" Comparison kicks in, the brain doesn't just record - it edits, frames, and assigns meaning. And finally, there's the symbolic layer, where archetypes, metaphors, and personal mythologies shape the story. A setback becomes a Hero's trial. A betrayal activates the Orphan. A breakthrough feels like the Visionary awakening.

Together, these layers transform raw data into felt experience. We don't just see - we interpret. We don't just hear - we assign meaning. We don't just feel - we narrate. And with narration, we create reality - our stories take on a life of their own.

This process is both automatic and trainable. With awareness, we can slow it down. We can ask: What am I sensing? What emotion is present? What story am I telling? What archetype is active? In doing so, we reclaim owner/authorship. We shift from being shaped by experience to shaping it.

In coaching, this awareness is transformative. A client who feels stuck may be caught in a distorted narrative. By unpacking the layers - body, emotion, thought, symbol - we help them rewrite the story. In trading, this awareness is strategic. A trader who reacts impulsively may be processing from a perceptional threat filter. What are the likely consequences of this:

Poor decision making - Impulsive reactions may lead to entering or exiting trades without analysis.

Emotional trading - Decisions are driven by fear or anxiety rather than strategy.

Inconsistent results - Gains and losses become erratic due to lack of discipline.

Increased stress - Repeated impulsive actions amplify tension and reduce confidence.

Erosion of capital and confidence - Mistakes accumulate, creating a cycle of self-doubt.

We can work through this with NLP, Gestalt and Archetypal method. Ultimately, experience is not fixed - it's fluid. It's a co-creation between the world and the self. And when we understand how we process information internally, we gain the power to reshape our reality - not by changing what happens, but by changing how we meet it.

Representational Systems which are the ways our mind encodes, stores, and works with information by using the senses - primarily in the imagination.

In NLP (Neuro-Linguistic Programming), they refer to the internal modes we think in:

Visual – mental images including memories, colors, configuration, and imagined scenarios.

Example: Remembering the way a chart looked before a price breakout.

Auditory – internal dialog, sounds, voices, tones, and rhythms.

Example: Replaying a coach's advice in your head before entering a trade.

Kinesthetic – feelings, textures, movements, bodily sensations.

Example: Feeling a gut tension before clicking "Buy" or a sense of relief after closing a position.

Auditory Digital – internal dialogue, logic, lists, and analytical sequences.

Example: Running through a checklist of entry rules in your mind.

We use all of them, but individuals tend to favor one or two, shaping how they process information, make decisions, and store memories.

How our language reflects how we process internally

If we process information and memorize in the visual system we will use correlating words/phrases:

Sharp, clear, see, show, reveal, imagine, foggy, hazy; that's quite clear, I see what you mean, I went blank, let's cast some light on the subject, I am getting a new perspective. I see it this way.

In the auditory system - correlating words/phrases:

Sounds clear, listen, tune, loud; I hear you, that rings a bell, that sounds good to me, listen to yourself, I can tune in to what you are saying,

In the Kinesthetic system - correlating words/phrases:

Feel, touch, handle, grasp, pressure; this feels right to me, get a handle on it, do you grasp the concept,

Conclusion: Recognizing internal representational systems - how people internally code experience through visual, auditory, kinesthetic - is vital for deep, resonant communication. When we tune into someone's preferred system, we speak their sensory language, enhancing rapport and clarity. A visually oriented person might respond best to phrases like "I see what you mean," while a kinesthetic thinker may connect more with "That feels right." By matching these patterns, we not only foster emotional safety but also unlock richer understanding, allowing messages to land with precision and impact. It's not just about words - it's about meeting minds in their native terrain. This is an important step in building Rapport.

The Structure of our Experience

Every experience we have is shaped not just by what happens, but by the interpretations and meanings we assign to it. These internal narratives act as filters, coloring perception and triggering emotional responses - whether it's excitement, fear, shame, or joy. The meaning we give to an event "I failed" vs. "I learned" directly influences how we feel and, in turn, how we behave. This loop between interpretation, emotion, and action is at the heart of human experience. By becoming aware of the stories we tell ourselves, we gain the power to shift our emotional landscape and choose more empowering responses.

The chart below illustrates the nature of our internal processing. Depending on beliefs and perceptional filters we have in place, we interpret and make meaning of all the information we take in. As a result, we experience – we generate emotions which result in behavior.

You change a perceptional filter, and you will get a different result i.e. different emotions, different behavior.

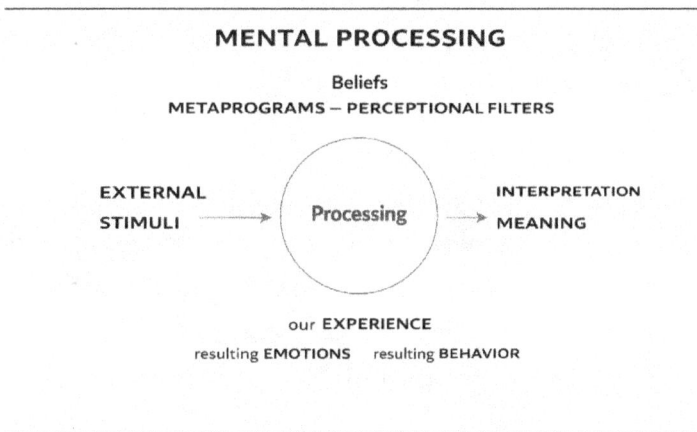

MENTAL PROCESSING

Beliefs
METAPROGRAMS – PERCEPTIONAL FILTERS

EXTERNAL   INTERPRETATION
STIMULI ⟶   Processing   ⟶   MEANING

our EXPERIENCE
resulting EMOTIONS   resulting BEHAVIOR

How Distorted Thinking appears in Language

Flawed or distorted thinking shows up in language mainly through Generalizations – Distortions – Deletions

Generalizations are mental shortcuts and one of the core processes by which we simplify and make sense of the world. This is an efficiency process of our brain. By grouping people, situations, or outcomes into broad categories, we risk overlooking nuance and individuality. We take a specific experience and apply its meaning broadly, often unconsciously. This can lead to rigid assumptions that limit understanding and create blind spots, especially when applied in areas that require careful judgment, such as relationships, decision-making, or problem-solving. Generalizations can also reinforce stereotypes, causing us to see what we expect instead of what is actually there. While these patterns are useful for learning, relying too heavily on them discourages curiosity and keeps us from seeing exceptions that might reveal new possibilities or insights.

Here are some linguistic clues. For example, someone who failed once might say, "I always mess things up," turning a single event into a sweeping identity statement. Here are the language cues – words such as: always, never, everyone, no one, all, none, every time, forever, constantly, only, totally, completely, absolutely, invariably, and automatically. In psychological contexts, they often signal cognitive distortions or limiting beliefs, such as "people always disappoint me," "I never succeed," or "nothing ever works."

NLP helps us spot these patterns in language and thought, then challenge them by asking precise questions that restore nuance and flexibility. These mental shortcuts - when left unchecked, can obscure possibility and reinforce limiting beliefs. Nobody likes me – people don' respects me. Generalizations can limit us by oversimplifying complex situations, or ideas, leading to biased thinking and missed opportunities. When we assume something is always true based on limited experience, we may ignore individual differences or new information. This will hinder personal growth, reduce empathy, and prevent meaningful connections or innovative solutions.

In trading, generalizations can be especially costly because markets are dynamic and rarely follow simple rules. Relying on broad assumptions like "this pattern always leads to profits" or "the market always reacts this way" can blind traders to unique conditions and shifting contexts. Such thinking reduces flexibility, encourages overconfidence, and may cause missed signals that contradict the generalization. Successful trading requires awareness of nuance, adaptability, and the discipline to test assumptions against real data rather than relying on oversimplified rules.

Now what to do since we built these patterns over time and turned them into habits of thinking being on full automation? This book will provide a learning context for sharpening your awareness and to deal effectively with generalizations. Stay tuned!

Distortions in our thinking are subtle shifts in perception that shape how we interpret reality, often bending facts to fit our beliefs, and arise from fears, or unmet needs. These mental habits show up in patterns like assuming we know what others are thinking, believing someone else controls our emotions, or turning dynamic experiences into rigid labels like "failure" or "success." Such distortions are clues for the coach to how meaning is being constructed. With awareness, we can challenge these patterns, reframe limiting narratives, and reclaim choice in how we respond to life's complexity. Whether it is in trading, coaching or therapy we want to revert from something static and unmovable back to an ongoing process. Let's differentiate between:

Cognitive Distortions: **Catastrophizing** is a cognitive distortion where we automatically expect the worst-case scenario to unfold, often exaggerating the potential negative impact of events. **Black and White thinking** is a cognitive distortion where situations, outcomes, or people are viewed in extremes, with no middle ground. In trading, this might show up as seeing a trade as either a complete success or total failure, ignoring nuanced outcomes or partial gains.
Personalization is a cognitive distortion where we take external events or others' actions as a reflection of ourselves, even when there's no direct connection. In trading, this might look like blaming oneself for every market loss or assuming that others' successes diminish your own abilities. Recognizing personalization helps separate personal identity from external

outcomes, allowing more objective decision-making and emotional balance.

Perceptual distortions

occur before meaning is made, at the level of what is noticed, filtered, amplified, or ignored. Our senses or interpretations of reality are altered by emotions, expectations, or past experiences, leading us to perceive situations in a biased or inaccurate way. They shape how we perceive others, ourselves, and events - often causing us to react to our interpretations rather than to what is actually happening. In short: Sensory input is misinterpreted.

Seeing volatility as "danger" when emotionally activated, and as "opportunity" when confident. Misreading a chart because your mind fills in patterns that aren't actually there.

Emotional distortions occur when feelings are amplified, misdirected, or outdated, causing the intensity or quality of an emotion to no longer match the present reality.

In trading they can tilt decision-making: fear can turn neutral market signals into perceived threats, prompting premature exits or hesitation. Greed amplifies potential rewards while minimizing risk, and euphoria after wins can foster overconfidence and excessive risk-taking. Regret keeps a trader fixated on missed opportunities or past mistakes, distracting from present-moment clarity and sound judgment.

Deletions in our language are the invisible edits we make when we speak or think - leaving out key details, assumptions, or emotional nuances. They help us communicate efficiently, by removing unnecessary details and focusing on the core message. In everyday conversation, we often leave out information that is assumed to be understood by the listener, which speeds up communication. However, if overused or used in the wrong context, deletions can also lead to misunderstandings or ambiguity. They also shape how we experience reality. For example, saying "I feel bad" omits why we feel bad, what triggered it, and what "bad" even means. These gaps can obscure clarity, reinforce vague discomfort, or limit our ability to respond effectively. By gently unpacking what's missing - asking questions like "about what" or "compared to what" You can also redirect into an outcome-oriented questions "What would you like to feel instead" thereby restoring depth, personal power, put you in the driver seat, bring the full picture back into view and reconnect with the whole experience by restoring clarity and context

In trading, deletions can subtly distort decision-making by omitting critical information from our internal dialogue or market analysis. A trader might say "The market's crashing" without specifying which asset, timeframe, or context - leading to reactive choices based on vague fear rather than precise data. Deletions also show up in self-talk like "I can't trade well," which skips over when, why, or under what conditions performance falters. By identifying what's missing - whether it's emotional nuance, technical detail, or contextual clarity - traders can reduce impulsivity, improve pattern recognition, and make more grounded, strategic decisions.

Self-Concept and identity

are the twin mirrors through which we perceive ourselves and shape our place in the world, They evolve over time, influenced by experience, the meaning we make, reflection, and relationship. How we are seen, named, and responded to by others becomes internalized, quietly forming the boundaries of who we believe we are and what we believe is possible.

At its core, **Self-Concept** is the self-sense we hold of who we are - our traits, roles, values, and beliefs. It's the internal voice which declares who I am such as , "I am a loyal person - I am resilient – I am analytical - I tend to be patient - I'm someone who likes structure," and it's built from the countless interactions and interpretations we gather throughout life. This concept does not remain static; it shifts as we grow, learn, and encounter new perspectives. In early childhood, we begin to recognize ourselves as distinct beings - what psychologists call the existential self. Soon after, we start categorizing ourselves: by gender, age, abilities, and affiliations. These layers form the categorical self, helping us navigate social roles and expectations.

Identity, meanwhile, is the broader narrative we construct about who we are and who we're becoming. Identity is a dynamic synthesis of self-perception and social reflection, shaped by memory, emotion, culture, and context – it is the interplay between inner coherence **and external adaptation across time, roles, and relationships**. As social actors, we perform roles and express traits in the presence of others. As motivated individuals, we pursue goals and values that reflect our inner desires. And as autobiographical authors, we weave our past, present, and imagined future into a coherent life story. This narrative identity is deeply personal yet shaped by culture, community, and context. It's where our self-concept meets meaning : "I am a leader – problem solver – a professional trader."

This congruence between our self-image and our ideal self can foster confidence and well-being, while dissonance may lead to inner conflict or growth. Humanistic psychologist Carl Rogers emphasized this dynamic, suggesting that a healthy self-concept arises when our self-image aligns with our lived experience and aspirations.

Ultimately, self-concept and identity are the basis of our humanity. They guide our choices, color our relationships, and shape how we interpret the world. To know oneself is to engage in an ongoing dialogue between who we are, who we've been, and who we're becoming. And in that dialogue, we find not just clarity but connection.

The Nature of Beliefs

How we Develop Beliefs

Beliefs are cognitive constructs they are the stories we tell ourselves about how the world works. They're shaped by a repetition of general experience, compelling reference experiences, culture, and conditioning. Some beliefs empower us , "I grow through challenge", while others limit us "I'm only valuable when I win".

Beliefs are reactive. They often arise from survival strategies or inherited scripts. They feed us predictions, assumptions, and judgments. And because they're often subconscious, they can quietly sabotage our goals - even when our intentions are noble.

Meta Programs

Our meta programs act like unconscious filters that shape how we interpret the world, and they are deeply intertwined with our beliefs. Beliefs then form within those filters. They explain and justify why the world appears the way it does through those same lenses. While beliefs form the content of what we hold to be true about ourselves, others, and reality, meta programs govern the structure of how we process that information - whether we focus on opportunities or problems, seek similarity or difference, move toward goals or away from risks. Over time, repeated patterns of attention and behavior reinforce certain beliefs, and those beliefs in turn strengthen the underlying meta programs, creating a self-reinforcing loop. By bringing awareness to this connection, we can see how much of what feels like "truth" is actually a product of our habitual ways of filtering experience, and we gain the possibility of shifting both the filters and the beliefs they sustain. You will be familiarized with some of the major Meta Programs later in this book.

"What Portion of your experience are you paying attention to!"

Part II - The Psychology of Markets and Traders

The markets are not just a mechanical system of numbers and charts - they are a living, breathing reflection of human psychology at scale. Every tick on the screen is the result of countless decisions made by individuals and institutions, each influenced by fear, greed, hope, uncertainty, and bias. Despite all the algorithms and tools, we have available, price movements are less about cold logic and more about the **"collective emotional state of participants"**. Euphoria inflates bubbles, panic accelerates crashes, and herd behavior drives trends far beyond what fundamentals justify. In this sense, trading is not simply about predicting patterns - it is about understanding how human minds react under pressure, and how those reactions shape the very patterns traders seek to exploit. Mastering the psychological nature of markets starts with mastering both your own decision-making process and your ability to read the emotions embedded in price action.

How cognitive biases sabotage even skilled traders

Even the most technically skilled traders are not immune to the invisible traps set by their own minds. Cognitive biases - mental shortcuts our brains use to process information - can quietly distort decision-making, leading to costly errors. Confirmation bias can make a trader see only the chart patterns that support their existing view while ignoring contradictory signals. Anchoring can cause them to fixate on a past price level, refusing to adapt as market conditions change. Loss aversion can push them to hold onto losing trades far too long, while the illusion of control can tempt them into overtrading, believing they can "command" the market into compliance. These biases operate beneath conscious awareness, meaning that traders can execute a well-tested strategy flawlessly in backtests but fall apart in live markets when emotions trigger these mental blind spots. Recognizing and neutralizing these biases is a survival skill.

Why NLP is a perfect fit for traders

Trading success depends less on predicting the market and more on managing the trader's own mental and emotional state, and this is exactly where Neuro-Linguistic Programming (NLP) excels. NLP offers practical tools for identifying thought patterns, beliefs, and emotional triggers that drive trading behavior, often outside conscious awareness. By learning to reframe setbacks, anchor confidence on-demand, and replace limiting self-talk with empowering mental scripts, traders can execute their strategies with greater discipline and consistency. Unlike generic trading psychology advice, NLP goes beyond theory and provides specific, actionable techniques to rewire the brain for peak performance under pressure. For traders facing the constant uncertainty of the markets, NLP is not just a performance enhancer - it is a mental operating system that can turn a good strategy into a consistently profitable one.

The Trader's Brain

Decision-making under uncertainty

Trading is the ultimate exercise in decision-making under uncertainty. No matter how much research you've done, every trade is a leap into the unknown, where probabilities - not certainties - govern the outcome. This constant ambiguity activates the brain's survival systems, often triggering fear, hesitation, or impulsive action. Faced with incomplete information, traders may overanalyze in search of a "perfect" signal that never comes, or they may rush into trades to avoid missing out. The challenge is not just reading the market - it's making clear, confident decisions when the future is unknowable, and the risk of loss is real. Developing the ability to act decisively, manage risk, and adapt quickly in the face of uncertainty is what separates consistently profitable traders from those who are perpetually paralyzed or reactive.

Fight-or-Flight and the Impact of Stress on Execution:

In trading, sudden market moves can trigger the body's fight-or-flight response, flooding the system with adrenaline and cortisol. While this reaction evolved to help us survive physical threats, in the market it often hijacks rational thinking, narrowing focus, speeding up decisions, and pushing traders toward impulsive actions. Under stress, discipline breaks down - plans are abandoned, rules are bent, and emotional trades replace strategic execution. Learning to recognize and regulate this physiological response is essential for maintaining clarity and sticking to a well-defined trading plan.

In a game where most participants are ruled by fear, greed, and impatience, emotional regulation becomes a trader's hidden edge. The ability to stay calm during drawdowns, resist euphoria after big wins, and make decisions based on process rather than impulse allows a trader to operate when others are self-sabotaging. By keeping emotions in check, you not only protect your capital - but you also position yourself to spot and seize opportunities that emotionally reactive traders will miss.

Emotions

Using Inner States in Service of Your Outcome

Emotions are our bodies intelligence officers, trying to communicate with the mind. Many people confuse emotions as the cause of problems, but they are not the enemy of reason but signal carriers.

When you strip away judgment, emotions are simply data - signals that reveal the quality of your current alignment with what matters most to you. They tell you where attention is flowing, what meaning you're assigning to events, and whether your current state supports or sabotages your desired outcome.

Yet most people treat emotions reactively suppressing, avoiding, or being consumed by them. In doing so, they lose access to their informational value. The key is not to control or eliminate emotions, but to decode them. Therefore I strongly suggest that you embrace them.

By treating emotions as feedback, you shift from victim of emotion to observer of signals. You begin to understand what your inner system is trying to tell you about your relationship to your goal. Awareness is the hinge between emotion and performance.

Emotional Energy as Directional Force

Once decoded, emotional energy can be rechanneled toward purposeful action.

Instead of suppressing fear, translate it into focus. Instead of resisting frustration, use its momentum to refine your process. The same energy that derails performance, when reoriented, fuels precision, creativity, and persistence.

E-motion is simply **energy in motion** - and energy becomes powerful when given direction.

True mastery is emotional integration - allowing emotions to exist without letting them define you.

You observe them, listen, learn, and redirect. When emotions serve your outcome, they become allies rather than adversaries. You evolve from emotional reactivity to emotional leadership.

In the end, emotions are not obstacles to performance - they are instruments of awareness. When tuned correctly, they guide you toward congruence, precision, and purpose.

Emotional Regulation as a Competitive Edge

Emotional regulation is one of the most overlooked yet powerful edges a trader can cultivate. Markets are designed to provoke fear, greed, and impatience - emotions that push traders toward impulsive decisions and away from disciplined strategy. The ability to regulate emotional responses under stress allows a trader to remain objective, stick to their process, and **make decisions based on probabilities** rather than impulses. Unlike technical indicators or market models, this edge cannot be easily copied; it's an internal skill that compounds over time. By mastering emotional regulation, traders preserve capital during volatile swings, avoid overtrading, and create the consistency necessary for long-term success.

When Emotions Create Blind Spots

Emotions are intelligent messengers - signals that point to something we need to notice. But when those emotions go unexamined, they start shaping how we see reality instead of informing it. What we feel begins to dictate what we perceive.

Under emotional pressure, the mind stops being curious and becomes defensive. Fear narrows vision - this can manifest as tunnel focus - where a trader fixates on a single price movement, indicator, or emotion, losing sight of the larger strategy or market structure. Pride filters feedback as a mask that hides truth, and Frustration compresses perspective. In that moment, the mind isn't seeking truth - it's seeking relief. It recruits logic not to explore reality, but to protect the feeling it identifies with, e.g. protect ego after wins or losses, block feedback that threatens self-image, reframe mistakes as justified or externalized.

This is how mental blind spots form: not from ignorance, but from emotional over-identification.

Awareness clears that fog. The simple shift from "I am anxious" to "I notice I'm anxious" reclaims space between emotion and identity. In that space, options return. Clarity re-emerges. The self becomes fluid again.

Emotional Safety in Trading: The Invisible Edge

In the high-stakes world of trading, emotional safety is often the missing variable - unseen, unmeasured, yet profoundly influential. While charts, algorithms, and macroeconomic indicators dominate the conversation, the trader's inner landscape - how safe they feel. This ties again into the self-feeding loops of CCC described in the opening page.

Emotional states are rarely mapped. And yet, it is this terrain that determines whether a trader can act with clarity, recover from losses, and evolve through uncertainty.

What Is Emotional Safety

We want to be in the driver seat and take action to create the space for emotional safety, a felt sense that one's emotions, intuitions, and cognitive processes are welcome - not punished. It's the permission to be human in a domain that often demands machine-like precision. In trading, this means:

- ➤ Psychological permission to feel - without shame or suppression.
- ➤ Relational trust - with mentors, teams, or oneself, to process mistakes and insights.
- ➤ Cognitive spaciousness - to explore multiple perspectives without fear of ridicule.
- ➤ Somatic regulation - tools to soothe the body when markets trigger stress responses.

The Cost of Unsafe Spaces

The cost of unsafe spaces shows up both internally and externally. Internally, it creates self-doubt, fear of failure, and inhibited growth, as individuals censor thoughts and emotions e.g. lack of authenticity. Externally, unsafe environments - whether in teams, organizations, or markets - stifle collaboration, trust, and innovation, leading to miscommunication, conflict, and missed opportunities.

When emotional safety is absent, traders may:

- ➤ Overreact to market volatility, mistaking fear for signal.
- ➤ Hide mistakes, avoiding post-mortems that could foster growth.
- ➤ Default to rigid strategies, unable to adapt under pressure.
- ➤ Internalize losses as personal failures, eroding self-trust.

In unsafe environments - whether internal (self-talk) or external (team culture) - the nervous system contracts.

Risk becomes threat. Curiosity collapses into control. And the trader, once a creative strategist, becomes a reactive survivor.

Micro-Moments That Build Safety

Emotional safety is cultivated through micro-moments. In trading, safety isn't about the market - it's about the mind. The most consistent traders aren't those who avoid risk, but those who create a stable inner environment that allows them to stay grounded under pressure. This stability is built through micro-moments of self-regulation and awareness repeated throughout the day.

Small shifts in practice ripple into deeper changes in self-perception. The trader begins to experience themselves not only as someone who acts, but someone who develops and learns. The role expands from executing risk to embodying insight, from chasing outcomes to creating significant structures. When reviewing performance with curiosity instead of judgment, creating space for learning will become possible rather than self-attack.

Emotional filters

Constructive emotional filters help traders perceive markets through a lens of possibility rather than threat.

They can shape how you interpret market signals.

Constructive filters such as curiosity, confidence, calm, and commitment expand perception and activate resourceful trading states and that is where you want to be - in an empowering internal state.

Limiting filters like fear, greed, frustration, shame and upsets narrow your focus and distort your interpretation of the market.

By noticing which emotional filter is active and which archetype is shaping your inner narrative, you gain the ability to shift the story - moving from threat-driven reactions to grounded, intentional trading behavior.

Utilizing Constructive Emotional Filters

Constructive emotional filters help the trader interpret uncertainty without distortion. Instead of reacting to fear or excitement, they translate emotional signals into information: Am I within my rules? Is my risk fixed? Is my state stable enough to execute? In this way, emotion becomes feedback for process, not a trigger for action. Let's have a more detailed look at emotions that help us expand perception, promote flexibility, and activate internal resources.

1. Curiosity

Trading State: Neutral, observational, data driven.

Symbolic/Archetypal Layer: The Explorer - seeking patterns, learning from the market without attachment.

Effect: Encourages experimentation, patient analysis, and openness to new setups.

2. Confidence

Trading State: Clear execution, trust in process, stable emotions and stable risk-taking.

Symbolic Layer: The Warrior - disciplined, prepared, acting with clarity rather than aggression.

Effect: Allows decisive action without emotional flooding.

3. Calmness

Trading State: Balanced presence, high focus, long-term perspective.

Symbolic Layer: The Sage - reflective, steady, internally anchored.

Effect: Reduces reactivity and overtrading, maintains consistent behavior.

4. Determination / Commitment

Trading State: Staying with the plan during drawdowns.

Symbolic Layer: The Builder - constructing over time, tolerating friction.

Effect: Helps navigate setbacks without abandoning strategy.

Constricting Emotional Filters

These emotions will narrow our perception, distort market signals, and trigger threat-based reactions. These are the emotions we want to transform – keep what's contextual useful and let go of what's limiting. Again our brain is wired for survival, anything perceived as a threat will activate these emotions.

1. Fear / Anxiety

Trading State: Avoidance, hesitation, premature exits.

Symbolic Layer: The Orphan - feels unsupported, expects harm or loss.

Effect: Sees threats everywhere; interprets normal volatility as danger.

2. Greed / Impulsivity

Trading State: Chasing trades, oversized positions, euphoria-driven risk.

Symbolic Layer: The Addict - seeks intensity, reward, and immediacy.

Effect: Overfocus on potential gain while ignoring risk signals.

3. Frustration / Anger

Trading State: Revenge trading, forcing outcomes.

Symbolic Layer: The Destroyer - reacts to perceived injustice or loss of control.

Effect: Collapses discipline and distorts objectivity.

4. Shame / Self-doubt

Trading State: Paralysis, inability to trust any decision.

Symbolic Layer: The Wounded Child - believes mistakes define identity.

Effect: Overly critical internal dialogue, emotional withdrawal, underperformance.

Emotional Consequences from a prolonged period of underperformance

A prolonged period of underperformance in trading can have far-reaching consequences besides affecting results - it slowly reshapes the trader. Confidence erodes, emotions become heavier, and decision-making grows distorted, leading to strategy/style drift, hesitation, or impulsive actions. Over time, traders may question their identity, lose motivation, and disconnect from routines or support systems. Financial pressure adds another layer of stress, pushing them into a defensive, survival-oriented mindset. In essence, extended underperformance impacts not only performance metrics but the trader's psychology, behavior, and sense of self. For this reason we need to be prepared to create safe zones.

Consistency as Mirror of Inner Alignment

When belief systems, goals, and values are aligned, discipline stops being a daily battle. Instead, it becomes a natural extension of identity – a way of being. Professionals act with consistency not because they "have to" but because it reflects who they are. For asset management firms and financial institutions, this translates into fewer costly errors, stronger collaboration, and a culture where performance is not only high but also sustainable.

In fast-moving markets, alignment between internal and external drivers is one of the most underleveraged competitive edges. When volatility spikes and decisions compress into seconds, most traders default to reactive mode - chasing price, scanning headlines, or clinging to outdated setups. But the real edge lies in congruence: the ability to align your internal drivers (values, emotional state, cognitive clarity) with external signals (price action, macro context, volatility regime).By investing in the integration of belief systems with professional goals and firm values, organizations can transform discipline from a fragile trait into a resilient standard.

Market Illusions - Cognitive Biases – Distorted Thinking

Fixations, Confirmation Bias, and Loss Aversion

Three of the most influential psychological traps in trading are anchors (fixations, attachments) confirmation bias, and loss aversion. This form of anchoring occurs when traders fixate on a specific price level - such as the entry price or a recent high - and allow it to distort their judgment, even when market conditions have clearly shifted. Confirmation bias drives traders to seek out only the information that supports their existing market view, blinding them to warning signs and alternative scenarios. Loss aversion, perhaps the most dangerous of all, causes traders to avoid taking small, planned losses, often turning manageable setbacks into catastrophic drawdowns. Together, these biases can lock traders into poor positions, delay necessary decisions, and erode discipline, ultimately undermining even the most robust trading strategies.

Perceived Cause-Effect relationships – Limiting Beliefs

Perceived C/E relationships are the connections we believe exist between events, even when the link is subjective or only partially true. We use them as mental shortcuts: "If X happens, then Y must follow." While these assumptions can help us navigate complexity quickly, they often oversimplify reality and shape our behavior in limiting ways. When left unexamined, they can turn into rigid rules filtering how we interpret situations, respond to challenges, or predict outcomes, even when the actual causation is far more nuanced.

Limiting beliefs are deeply held assumptions we accept as truth that restrict our potential and choices. They often develop from past experiences, social conditioning, or fear of failure, and they quietly shape how we see ourselves and what we believe is possible. Again, if we leave them unchallenged, these beliefs act like invisible barriers, holding us back from growth and preventing us from taking opportunities that could lead to success or fulfillment. One of our most common mental flaws is drawing incorrect cause-effect relationships.

It is a mental shortcoming – to assume that because one event follows another, the first must have caused the second – this can be a subtle but costly trap for traders. For example, a trader might notice that every time a particular news outlet releases a bullish headline, the market seems to rise shortly after, leading them to believe the headline is driving the move. In reality, both events could be reacting to a separate underlying factor, or the correlation could be pure coincidence. This false cause-effect thinking can lead traders to build strategies on unreliable patterns, chase meaningless signals, and misinterpret market drivers. Recognizing and avoiding the "after the fact fallacy" is essential for basing trading decisions on robust evidence rather than seductive but misleading narratives.

We want to have accuracy and precision to avoid mental barriers that can stop someone from taking risks, trying new things, or believing in their own potential.

Logical level models tied to Cause/Effect

In the Logical Levels framework, our beliefs about cause-and-effect act as powerful organizing forces. They determine how we interpret events, assign responsibility, and make meaning across the different layers of our self-concept and identity - from environment and behavior up to capabilities, values, and purpose. When these cause/effect connections are rigid or distorted, they can trap us in non-useful mental/behavioral loops. By exploring how we structure these causal links within each logical level, we gain the ability to challenge limiting interpretations and create more empowering relationships between what happens and what it means for who we are and what we can do.

Originally developed by Gregory Bateson and expanded by Robert Dilts in NLP, the Logical Levels model organizes human experience into a hierarchy: environment (where and when we act), behavior (what we do), capabilities (how we do it), beliefs and values (why we do it or not), identity (who we are as a result of a few generalizations we make), and spirituality or purpose (for whom or what we serve).

When applying the Logical Levels framework, the key is to intervene at the level where the resistance is anchored in order to restore movement and choice. Each level holds a different type of blockage - behavioral habits, missing capabilities, limiting beliefs, identity conflicts, or purpose misalignment - and change will only be sustainable when the intervention matches the level at which the system is stuck. Interventions at the wrong level may create temporary compliance, but intervening at the right level creates lasting transformation.

Behavioral difficulties usually signal deeper issues. Patterns like procrastination or ineffective communication are rarely rooted in the behavior itself; they typically trace back to limiting beliefs "I'm not capable," "If I speak up, people will think I'm stupid," "I'm not someone who succeeds" or "My team doesn't support me."

Working only at the surface level (behavior) might temporarily change actions, but without addressing the underlying structure (beliefs, values, identity), the change is fragile or short-lived.

Common limiting perceived cause-effect beliefs often arise when people assume that one external factor automatically dictates their inner state or capabilities, such as "If the market moves against me, it means I am not skilled," or "If others don't approve, I cannot succeed," or "It's wrong to be assertive"

These beliefs distort reality because **they commingle correlation with causation** and restrict personal choice. On the environment level, they can make people feel powerless, attributing outcomes solely to external conditions. On the behavior level, they lead to avoidance or overcompensation, narrowing the range of possible actions. At the capability level, they erode confidence by suggesting skills are ineffective or predetermined by circumstances. At the identity level, they can crystallize into harmful self-concepts, such as "I am a failure." And at the level of purpose or values, they may create dissonance, causing individuals to abandon pursuits that once felt meaningful. Differentiating these beliefs across logical levels allows us to see how a single distorted cause-effect link can cascade through multiple layers of experience, limiting growth and potential. Each level shapes the others, and meaningful change often requires working at the deeper levels rather than only addressing surface actions. Now let's relate to these logical levels in more depth.

Environmental/Behavioral

When traders operate in a focused, well-equipped environment (quiet space, reliable tech, supportive community), they tend to engage in more disciplined behaviors.

Distractions or chaotic surroundings disrupt the internal conditions required for clear, disciplined trading. When the environment is cluttered, unstable, or demanding, traders become more susceptible to impulsive actions, missed setups, and emotionally driven decisions. But the "environment" isn't limited to what's around you; it also includes what you carry within you.

Inner turbulence can produce the same lack of results just like external chaos. A poor night's sleep, unresolved tension with a partner/children, lingering stress, or mental overload can narrow perceptual bandwidth and weaken emotional regulation. As a result, decision quality deteriorates. What looks like a "trading mistake" is often a reflection of a compromised internal environment.

My trading decisions were flawed today not because the market behaved unpredictably, but because I entered the session already depleted. Unresolved concerns pulled my focus away from the charts. I wasn't fully present, therefore my precision and execution suffered.

When viewing in this context, trading errors are not isolated events they are downstream expressions of your overall state and environment, both outer and inner. Managing both is essential to sustaining consistency and precision. "The market news caused me to lose money." In this case external context (news) are blamed for personal behavior (trading decisions).

Another example is to link "Anchors of your Sense of Success" on age or timelines, rather than effort, adaptability and evolution that truly define growth. These anchors act like invisible rules thereby shaping how we evaluate progress and worth. This mindset creates pressure and false comparisons, ignoring the diverse and nonlinear paths people can take. A more meaningful anchor for success is steady progress, resilience, and continuous learning, which build sustainable achievements regardless of when they occur. While they may be temporary motivating, but in the long run fostering a distorted view of what is actually possible.

Consistent behaviors like journaling, following routines, and reviewing trades build skill over time.

Erratic or reactive behaviors prevent traders from developing the pattern recognition and emotional regulation needed for mastery.

Capability

As you sharpen your skills in risk management, strategic execution, and adaptability, these capacities will gradually become second nature - shaping a new, integrated identity as a trader. Competence reinforces self-beliefs like "I am a strategic risk-taker" or "I'm becoming a professional," while repeated failure without reflection can erode confidence and identity. The following examples illustrate how this shapes a person's mindset, productivity, and overall success.

"If I haven't succeeded by now, I never will."

"If I can't predict this stock, it means I'll never be successful."

Skill limitations in one area are incorrectly elevated into a belief about success.

Conclusion: "Capability isn't proven by a single outcome - it develops through mindful pattern repetition, sustained effort, and time. One moment of success may inspire, but it's the rhythm that reveals depth." A single failure does not define your ability or who you are.

In our coaching sessions we keep skills (trainable) separate from identity-defining beliefs.

Identity:

In the Logical Levels model, the cause/effect relationships we form don't just shape how we interpret events - they influence how we define who we are. When a trader links outcomes to identity through rigid causation "Because I made a mistake, I am undisciplined," or "Since I'm struggling right now, maybe I'm not a real trader" - behavioral setbacks become personal labels. These cause/effect links breakdown the separation between actions and identity, creating unnecessary self-limiting beliefs. By examining how we assign cause and meaning across the logical levels, we can separate temporary experiences from core identity, allowing performance issues to be addressed at the right level without turning them into identity statements.

A trader who identifies as disciplined will naturally act in ways that reinforce that identity - setting rules, respecting limits, and seeking growth.

Conversely, someone who sees themselves as impulsive or unlucky may unconsciously sabotage their own performance, creating a self-fulfilling cycle.

Here are some additional examples how this plays out in real life impacting performance and self-concept, when beliefs are misattributed to identity .

"Because I lost this trade, I'm a bad trader."

"Since I hesitated, I missed the trade therefore I'm indecisive."

"If I fail, it means I'm not good enough and I am a failure."

In this case one instance of behavior is generalized to define a person's identity.

Generally, if a person internalizes failure as a reflection of self-worth, it discourages risk-taking and learning.

Let's be clear: A single behavior doesn't determine a person's overall skill. Our capability is shown through patterns over time and not through isolated outcomes.

These statements show also the meta program all-or-nothing thinking and illustrate how confusing beliefs with identity can affect performance

"If I can't stay disciplined, I must not be cut out for this."

"The financial loss made me doubt the value of my efforts and what I'm doing with my life."

Equates momentary or short-term behavior with fixed capability or identity implications. A temporary identity experience is projected upward into life purpose.

Beliefs shape behavior, but they don't define who you are. Someone who avoids taking risks may simply hold the belief "I always mess things up," not an identity of being incompetent. A trader who hesitates to execute a plan might be driven by the belief "I can't trust myself," rather than an identity of being unreliable or flawed." Someone who is quiet in meetings may be reacting to the belief "My ideas aren't valuable," not an identity of having an inherent lack of confidence. When you separate beliefs from identity, behavior becomes something you can change - not a verdict on who you are

To summarize, beliefs shape behavior, but they don't equal who you are. You are not your money!

Your purpose is not determined by a single role or outcome.

Cultural:

Certain cultural narratives reflect limiting cause-and-effect assumptions that shape behavior. Beliefs like "If I don't follow the traditional path, I'll never succeed" close off alternative routes to growth and innovation. The idea that "If I show emotions, I'll seem weak" pressures people to suppress authenticity and emotional intelligence. Others fear that "If I take care of myself, people will think I'm selfish," which inhibits healthy boundaries and self-care. And the belief "If I don't make everyone happy, I've failed" fuels people-pleasing and self-abandonment. These perceived cultural linkages often restrict personal freedom rather than reflect reality.

Changing "Complex Equivalence"

In NLP this term describes a belief or assumption that two experiences or events are interpreted as meaning the same thing - even though that connection is subjective, not factual or evidence based. "She didn't call me back -therefore she doesn't care enough about me." Complex Equivalence shows up when someone says:

"I missed a trade - this proves I'm not disciplined."

"He disagreed with me - he could have shown more respect."

Each example ties one event to a general meaning, skipping over all other possible explanations. **This is the core process: the mind fuses an observable fact with an assumed meaning, turning a moment into a narrative.**

In trading, Complex Equivalence can be especially dangerous. A losing day may be interpreted as "I'm losing my edge," or market volatility might become "The market is out to get me." These interpretations instantly shape emotional state, decision-making, and ultimately performance. When left unchallenged, they can create loops of fear, frustration, or self-doubt. It also highlights why the way we apply language in our internal dialog is so powerful. We are creators or cause in the matter.

Becoming aware of Complex Equivalences helps traders and individuals separate what happened from what they're making it mean. Instead of collapsing experience into identity or emotional narratives, they gain the mental space to ask: Could this mean something else? What evidence do I actually have?

A failed trade is data - not destiny. Your edge lies in the discovery of patterns and adhering to a specific process, not the exception.

Here is another example that has impact on various levels and shows **the interconnection between Beliefs and Values**:

"If I speak up, people will think I'm stupid."

The speaker expresses a perceived consequence tied to an action ("speaking up") and a judgment about self-worth or social perception ("people will think I'm stupid").

It reflects an internalized belief about how others respond to one's behavior, which influences decision-making, emotional safety, and self-expression.

This belief may stem from past experiences, cultural conditioning, or identity-level hurts - but it operates as a filter that shapes behavior and limits potential.

How does this relate to other levels?

Behavior: It inhibits the act of speaking up.

Identity: If repeated or reinforced, it may evolve into "I am stupid" or "I'm not someone who speaks up e.g. I am shy" shifting into identity-level limitation. Spin it further and you may end up "I don't belong here – this is not my crowd, because I am not good enough".

Environment: The belief may be triggered or reinforced by specific social settings or relationships.

Capabilities: It may block the development or expression of communication skills or confidence.

Why these C/E Beliefs Are Limiting

They oversimplify reality and ignore context, complexity, and personal growth.

We often create broad generalizations from one powerful experience or from a few events that occurred under similar circumstances.

They're often also rooted in past emotional residue, unresolved situations, or societal conditioning.

They can block resilience, creativity, and self-compassion - all crucial for growth.

More about this in the "Reframing Chapter"

The Nature of Conflicting and Hierarchy of Criteria

In decision-making, conflicting criteria arise when two or more goals, values, or objectives cannot be fully satisfied at the same time. Every meaningful choice requires weighing trade-offs: optimizing one dimension often comes at the expense of another. For instance, a company may want to maximize product quality while also minimizing costs - two criteria that often pull in opposing directions. Similarly, an individual might value freedom while also craving security; pursuing one can sometimes undermine the other.

The presence of conflicting criteria is common - it is a natural condition in complex systems. In fact, recognizing these tensions is the first step toward more conscious choices. Attempting to satisfy every criterion equally often leads to paralysis or diluted outcomes. Instead, decision-makers benefit from identifying priorities, clarifying values, and accepting the compromises inherent in real-world choices.

Conflicting Criteria in Trading

The world of trading is a vivid example of decision-making under conflicting criteria. Traders constantly balance competing demands; each has its own logic and allure. Some of the most common conflicts include:

Risk vs. Reward: Higher potential returns usually involve higher risk, yet protecting capital requires restraint. Striking the right balance is a perpetual tension for traders.

Short-Term Gains vs. Long-Term Consistency: The lure of immediate profit can conflict with the discipline required to build sustainable returns over time.

Speed vs. Accuracy: Markets move quickly, and seizing opportunities often demands rapid action. But rushing decisions may compromise analysis and increase errors:

System Rules vs. Human Intuition: Many traders develop structured systems to reduce bias, yet moments arise when intuition suggests breaking the rules. The process of deciding when to trust often brings inner tension.

Independence vs. Market Consensus: Traders may seek to stand apart from the crowd to capture unique opportunities, yet ignoring collective signals can be costly.

Why These Conflicts Matter

Unresolved conflicting criteria can lead to indecision, impulsive reactions, or overcorrection. A trader who constantly shifts between maximizing gains and minimizing losses may end up achieving neither, creating a cycle of frustration and inconsistency. On the other hand, those who acknowledge the inherent conflicts and deliberately choose how to resolve them are better equipped to act with clarity and resilience. In trading, stress often arises when multiple priorities or values pull in different directions. Traders constantly balance conflicting criteria: pursuing high returns versus managing risk, acting quickly versus ensuring thorough analysis, or sticking to strategy versus responding to market volatility. When these objectives clash, decision-making can feel overwhelming and can be stressful.

Values and Conflicting Criteria

Values play a central role in how conflicting criteria are experienced and resolved, because they act as the deeper compass guiding our choices. When two criteria are in conflict - such as safety versus growth, or freedom versus stability - the tension often reflects an underlying clash between the values they represent. In these moments, decision-making is less about technical optimization and more about aligning choices with what matters most at a core level. The difficulty arises when **multiple values feel equally important**, leaving us torn between competing priorities. By clarifying and ranking our values, we can transform conflicting criteria from paralyzing dilemmas into conscious trade-offs, making decisions that are not only practical but also congruent with our sense of meaning and integrity.

Solutions for Conflicting Criteria

Navigating conflicting criteria in trading requires a blend of self-awareness, clearly defined principles, and adaptive flexibility. The most successful traders are not those who eliminate compromises but those who learn to live with them, using structure to anchor their decisions while leaving space for judgment and evolution.

In the end, both in life and in markets, conflicting criteria are less an obstacle than an invitation to refine priorities, deepen understanding, and grow in wisdom.

This layered approach helps individuals or teams prioritize what matters most - placing core values, strategic objectives, or non-negotiables at the top, followed by secondary considerations like feasibility, aesthetics, or convenience. By clarifying which criteria carry the most weight, the hierarchy streamlines complex choices, reduces cognitive overload, and fosters alignment across stakeholders. It's especially useful in coaching, design, or trading contexts where competing needs must be navigated with clarity and intention.

The "illusion of control" and overtrading - Risk

The "illusion of control" leads traders to believe they can influence or predict market outcomes far more than they actually can. This mindset often emerges after a streak of winning trades, creating a false sense of mastery that fuels excessive risk-taking. Convinced they can "read" the market, traders may increase position sizes, shorten their holding periods, or enter trades without proper setups -behaviors that quickly slide into overtrading. Each impulsive trade erodes discipline, exposes the account to unnecessary risk, and clouds judgment. Recognizing that the market is inherently unpredictable - and focusing instead on controlling only what truly can be controlled, such as risk management and process - helps traders avoid the destructive cycle of illusion-driven overtrading.

Perceived risk versus actual risk

Perceived risk in trading is shaped by emotion, bias, and incomplete information - while actual risk is grounded in data, structure, and uncertainty. The gap between them can distort decision-making and sabotage performance. It is the trader's internal narrative: the gut reaction, the fear spike, the memory of a past loss. Actual risk, by contrast, is the statistical probability of loss based on market structure, volatility, and position sizing. The problem - these two rarely align.

Having clear risk parameters means defining in advance how much capital you're willing to risk per trade, where your stop-loss levels are placed, and what conditions justify exiting a position. This structure protects you from emotional decision-making and ensures consistency, even in volatile markets. It transforms risk from a vague fear into a manageable, strategic component of your trading plan.

Risk-Adjusted Position Sizing:

Before entering a trade, the trader calculates how much to put at risk based on account size and volatility.

Predefined Stop-Loss Discipline: The trader sets a stop-loss at X% below entry and stick to it, even when the market dips and rebounds emotionally. They accept the loss and move on, preserving capital and mental clarity.

Predefined Re-Entry After a Stop Loss

A predefined re-entry is a planned and rule-based method for getting back into a trade after your stop loss has been hit, without emotional improvisation. Instead of treating a stopped-out trade as a failure, the trader anticipates the possibility of noise, shakeouts, or volatility spikes and prepares a second, higher-probability entry in advance.

Back Tested Strategy Execution: Using a proven setup - say, a moving average crossover with volume confirmation - the trader enters only when all conditions align. No chasing, no guessing. There is no guarantee that this setup will always be successful, but the correct setup will go a long way towards avoiding emotional pitfalls.

Now let's consider that there can be a significant difference between our perception and what real evidence is. Our key question needs to be: What is supporting my conclusions?

Factors influencing our perception of risk

Personal Experience

Past experiences with a particular risk can shape how it is perceived. For example, someone who has been in a car accident may perceive driving as riskier than someone who has not. My own compelling personal reference experience goes back to period of the Dot Com Bubble 2000 - 2002. I was still in the infancy of my trading and rather naïve. None of the procedures I have described in this book were in place and I didn't have a trader identity. After the NASDAQ had fallen by

37%, I assumed we must be nearly at the bottom and started to buy stocks in companies such as Enron, Global Crossing, WorldCom, Nortel and others. Since the great depression we had not experienced such a significant drop in an index. It was inconceivable for me that there could be a further significant drop. Here are some samples of my portfolio holdings at this time. **Enron** collapsed in December 2001 due to massive accounting fraud, where executives used complex, off-the-books partnerships to hide debt and inflate earnings, ultimately leading to the largest bankruptcy in U.S. history at the time.

Global Crossing experienced a major collapse and Chapter 11 bankruptcy filing in 2002 due to overbuilding a global fiber-optic network that exceeded demand and generated massive debt, a victim of the telecom bubble.

MCI WorldCom, a telecommunications giant that grew through acquisitions, collapsed in 2002 when it filed for Chapter 11 bankruptcy after an accounting scandal where executives hid billions in expenses to inflate profits. **Nortel Networks** collapsed due to financial mismanagement, accounting fraud, and the bursting of the dot-com bubble in the early 2000s, which led to enormous losses for customers and shareholders.

The NASDAQ had lost from March 2000 to October 2002 about 77% of its value.

This experience shaped my actions for many years to come. At the time I relied too much on press releases and analyst ratings, and some brokerage firms still had a buy rating on these issues. I was also fixated on historical prices, had too much sector exposure and poor risk management. After those events, my trading decisions became hesitant, my risk tolerance shrank, and I began passing on strong setups - taking profits too early and consistently leaving the upside on the table.. Situations like this are a major invitation for qualified coaching.

Choice and Voluntariness

Risks taken voluntarily are often seen as less severe than those imposed. Let's say you are a trader in a financial institution, and your superior instructs you to take over someone else's book.

Media Influence

Media coverage can greatly impact how risks are perceived. High-profile news stories about rare but dramatic events can lead to overestimation of those risks.

Familiarity

Risks that are well-known and understood are often perceived as less dangerous than unfamiliar ones. For instance, trading a strategy or an instrument you're familiar with.

Social and Cultural Factors

Cultural beliefs and social norms can shape how risks are perceived. Different cultures may have varying attitudes towards certain activities and their associated risks.

As we can see the illusion of control is closely related to what we belief. You will learn more about it in the chapter about beliefs.

The Illusion of Control

In trading, risk is often experienced not as an external market condition, but as something personal – as something that can be managed, reduced, or even eliminated through the trader's own actions. This is a powerful perception, and it can also be misleading. While skill and discipline matter, uncertainty is part of the game. Yet the mind continuously searches for ways to feel in control.

Let's have a closer look how these illusions can be expressed and what underlying beliefs and presuppositions must be in place.

There is a belief that deeper analysis equals less risk. Traders who spend hours refining indicators or studying charts often increase position size, feeling that effort itself has created safety. In reality, analysis improves long-term edge, not the outcome of any single trade.

Another form appears in timing. Waiting for the perfect entry or exit creates the sense that precision can eliminate uncertainty. Stops are moved tighter, trades are monitored obsessively, and fast reactions are mistaken for control. What is actually happening is an attempt to outmaneuver randomness.

Attention becomes another substitute for control. Many traders feel safer when watching a trade tick by tick, even though their presence has no influence on price. The screen becomes a psychological anchor.

Rules and systems can also create a false sense of certainty. A strategy that worked in one market may not work if market regime changes and yet is blindly trusted. Winning streaks justify oversized positions. Rules are followed not to manage risk, but to quiet anxiety. One thing we can say with certainty **Structure** reduces emotional chaos, yet uncertainty remains.

For experienced traders, identity itself can becomes a source of illusion. "I am disciplined" or "I've been doing this for years" replaces proper risk assessment. Losses are held longer to protect self-image, not capital.

Perhaps the most dangerous illusion appears after loss: the belief that risk can be repaired. Adding to losers, revenge trading, or reframing emotional reactions as strategy are all attempts to restore a sense of equilibrium. Don't confuse recovery with control.

Control becomes the emotional substitute for certainty - and discipline begins when this illusion is seen clearly, not when it is perfected.

The Solution:

Shift from Outcome Control to Process Control - Where control truly lives in Trading.

Every trader eventually confronts the same uncomfortable truth: the market cannot be controlled. Price will do what it does, when it does it. No amount of analysis, attention, speed, or experience can eliminate uncertainty. Many of the psychological traps in trading arise from trying to control the wrong thing - outcomes.

When traders believe they can personally control risk, they develop subtle illusions. They analyze more, time entries more precisely, watch the screen more closely, or rely on systems as if structure could remove randomness. These behaviors are understandable and are attempts to reduce helplessness. When you fight reality you will exhaust discipline.

The solution is not to abandon control - it is to relocate it.

Professional traders learn to move control away from the market and into the process. They stop trying to manage price and start managing conditions. Position size is decided before entry. Risk is fixed. Exits are defined when the mind is calm. Exposure is balanced across trades. The trader controls execution quality, not outcome.

This shift changes everything. When success is measured by process rather than profit, discipline becomes stable. A losing trade taken correctly is no longer a failure; it is evidence of learning and professionalism. A winning trade taken incorrectly becomes a warning, not a reward. Responsibility becomes clear, and anxiety drops.

Cognitive Biases

Cognitive biases distort our perception of market reality, leading us to make decisions based on emotion or flawed reasoning rather than objective analysis. Cognitive biases stem from deeply ingrained internal programs - mental shortcuts and emotional conditioning shaped by past experiences, beliefs, and survival instincts. In trading, these programs unconsciously influence how we interpret data, respond to risk, and justify decisions, often overriding rational analysis. Recognizing and reprogramming these patterns is key to developing emotional discipline and aligning behavior with strategic intent.

Here are some of the main culprits.

Optimism Bias: This is the tendency to overestimate the likelihood of positive outcomes while underestimating the chances of negative ones. This bias can lead to overly positive predictions and ignoring potential risks.

Catastrophizing - Worst-Case Scenario Bias:

Assuming bad things or the worst will happen such as a market crash.

Mental Shortcuts - Refer to where you rely on immediate examples that come to mind when evaluating a topic or making a decision. For instance, if you've recently heard about a plane crash in the news, you might think air travel is more dangerous than it actually is, simply because the crash is fresh in your memory.

Emotional bias – I feel it so strongly therefore I believe it must be true.

Fear, anxiety, and other emotions can lead to an overestimation of the likelihood and severity of risks. Emotions play a key role in risk perception

Trust

Trust in authorities, experts, and institutions can influence how risks are perceived. If people trust the source of information, they may perceive the risk as being less severe.

Since the main focus of this book is about mindset of the trader we will not dive into actual trading/market risks the trader faces.

Cognitive Dissonance in Trading

Cognitive dissonance in trading occurs when a trader's actions conflict with their beliefs or strategies, leading to mental discomfort and potentially poor decision-making. This happens when their beliefs, expectations, and actions are out of alignment - often under the pressure of risk, uncertainty, and money on the line. Here are some common scenarios where cognitive dissonance can arise in trading:

Conflicting Market Signals: When traders receive mixed signals from the market, they might struggle to decide whether to buy or sell, causing dissonance.

Emotional Attachments: Traders might become emotionally attached to a particular stock or trade, making it difficult to cut losses when necessary.

Confirmation Bias: Traders may seek out information that supports their existing beliefs and ignore contradictory data, leading to biased decision-making.

Rationalizing Losses: After a losing trade, traders might rationalize their decisions to avoid admitting mistakes, which can lead to repeated poor choices

Holding losing trades because "it will come back" (belief: "I'm a disciplined trader" vs. action: emotionally clinging to a position)

Overtrading after a loss (belief: "I follow my plan" vs. action: revenge trading).

Ignoring stops (belief: "risk management is key" vs. action: moving stops further away).

Cherry-picking trades (belief: "I trust my system" vs. action: skipping valid setups because of fear).

Staying in winning trades too long out of greed (belief: "I take profits at my targets" vs. action: waiting for more).

Rationalizing Losses: After a losing trade, traders might rationalize their decisions to avoid admitting mistakes, which can lead to repeated poor choices. You may be familiar with some of these experiences.

Why It Happens

Ego protection – admitting a wrong trade feels like admitting you are a bad trader.

Invested cost fallacy – unwillingness to let go because of time, money, or emotional investment.

Confirmation bias – seeking news or charts that support the current position, ignoring contradicting data.

Loss aversion – pain from loss outweighs pleasure from gain, distorting decisions.

Identity conflict – clash between "I am rational" and "I feel fear/greed."

Congruence vs. Incongruence

Congruence is essential in trading because it aligns internal beliefs, emotions, and actions - creating a coherent, grounded decision-making process that reduces self-sabotage and emotional whiplash. Its nature is integrative: when thoughts, feelings, and behaviors reflect a unified intent, traders can act with clarity, confidence, and resilience under pressure.

Internal Incongruence is the subtle yet powerful tension that arises when our thoughts, emotions, and actions fall out of alignment. Incongruence, by contrast, breeds hesitation, inner conflict, and reactive choices that undermine both strategy and self-trust. It's the dissonance between what we say and what we feel, between the roles we perform and the values we hold. Often, it manifests not as a loud crisis but as a quiet erosion - fatigue that lingers, motivation that falters, relationships that feel slightly off.

This misalignment can stem from external pressures, inherited beliefs, or unresolved inner conflicts. We may pursue goals that no longer resonate, speak words that betray our deeper truths, or maintain habits that contradict our evolving identity. Over time, these fractures accumulate, creating a sense of fragmentation that's difficult to name but impossible to ignore.

Here are some examples when a clash between beliefs and behavior occurs while the behavior does not match the value:

"I value honesty, but I just lied to protect someone, or to avoid confrontation."

"Eating healthy is important for my well-being, but I am regularly consuming fast food or sugary snacks."

"I need to save money to secure my future but frequently make impulsive purchases."

"I should only take trades with a clear edge. But jumping into high-risk trades based on emotions."

"I should only risk 1–2% of my account per trade but increase position size impulsively after a losing streak to win it back."

"I value patience and understanding but reacting angrily in stressful situations."

"I need to challenge myself to grow, but avoid new opportunities out of fear or laziness"

This ambivalence creates tension and will very likely trigger rationalization or avoidance as coping mechanisms. The trader might avoid reviewing losing trades or journaling because doing so would highlight repeated mistakes. These coping mechanisms reduce immediate discomfort but prevent learning, reinforce unhelpful habits, and disconnect actions from core values, ultimately increasing stress and undermining long-term performance. More about this in the chapter "Aligning Habits with your newly created identity"

Cognitive & Emotional Signs:

Saying "I'm fine" while visibly tense or withdrawn.

Laughing at something that actually feels hurtful.

Feeling drained after doing something that "should" feel fulfilling.

Avoiding decisions despite claiming clarity.

Overexplaining or justifying choices that don't sit well internally.

Somatic vs. Verbal Incongruence:

Body says one thing, words say another.

Smiling while expressing grief.

Using confident language with hesitant tone or body language

Making promises that evoke discomfort or resentment

Speaking in clichés or borrowed phrases that lack personal resonance.

Performing roles (leader, caregiver, expert) that feel misaligned or hollow.

Expressing values that contradict lived actions.

Physical & Somatic Indicators:

Chronic tension in the jaw, shoulders, or gut during certain conversations.

Restlessness or fatigue in environments that demand "enthusiasm".

Sudden emotional shifts - tears, irritability, numbness - without clear external cause.

Difficulty maintaining eye contact when discussing personal truths.

Additional Examples of Incongruence:

Your resist structure but crave impact.

I know I'm safe, but I still feel anxious.

Setting goals, avoiding action.

People-pleasing while resenting commitment.

Archetypes in Trading

Utilizing archetypes in trading coaching offers a powerful way to understand the deeper psychological patterns that drive decision-making, discipline, and risk-taking. Archetypes act as symbolic lenses through which traders can recognize recurring emotional states - such as the Hero's drive to conquer, the Caretaker's need for security, or the Trickster's impulse to outsmart the market. By identifying which archetypes are active in their behavior, traders gain access to the underlying motivations and fears shaping their performance. This awareness allows them to balance competing inner forces, transform self-sabotaging patterns, and engage the market with greater clarity, confidence, and authenticity.

Working with archetypes can be a very powerful way to achieve congruence. Here are some examples how archetypes in trading can appear. We have 2 inner figures pulling in opposite directions. Similar to Gestalt where we deal with polarities and in NLP with conflicting subpersonalities.

A note of caution: When working with Archetypes we want to make certain that we are utilizing the characteristics of Archetypal Strengths and not the Shadow Aspects.

Archetypal Conflicts

The Warrior vs. The Caregiver

Conflict: The Warrior archetype thrives on conquest, risk, and decisive action - driven to dominate the market and prove strength. The Caregiver, by contrast, seeks safety, preservation, and emotional harmony, often resisting aggressive moves or high-stakes trades.

Trading Impact: This conflict can lead to hesitation during volatile opportunities or self-sabotage after a win, as the trader unconsciously tries to "protect" themselves or others from perceived harm. It may also show up as guilt after taking profits while others lose.

The Magician vs. The Orphan

Conflict: The Magician archetype trusts intuition, transformation, and pattern recognition - believing in flow and synchronicity. The Orphan carries wounds of abandonment, betrayal, and skepticism, often expecting the market to punish or deceive.

Trading Impact: This tension can cause a trader to second-guess their edge, dismiss intuitive signals, or over-rely on rigid systems to avoid emotional vulnerability. It may also manifest as fear of trusting one's own evolution or success.

The Ruler vs. The Rebel

Conflict: The Ruler values structure, control, and mastery - seeking to govern the trading process with discipline and rules. The Rebel craves freedom, disruption, and innovation - resisting constraints and questioning authority.

Trading Impact: This inner clash can lead to rule-breaking, impulsive trades, or sabotage of well-crafted systems. The trader might alternate between over-control and reckless experimentation, struggling to find a rhythm that honors both order and originality.

Here is another example non trading related you may be familiar with:

The Lover wants connection; the Warrior demands boundaries.

Restoring Congruence

It starts with self-awareness, and you can begin noticing the subtle signals: the sigh before a meeting, the hesitation in a conversation, the recurring dream that doesn't quite make sense. These are invitations to realign, to listen inward, and to gently recalibrate. Whether through reflection, dialogue, or coaching, the path forward is one of integration - where inner truth and outer expression begin to harmonize.

In a world that often rewards performance over authenticity, tending to internal congruence is a radical act of self-respect. It's not just about feeling better - it's about becoming whole.

Meta-Program Misalignments

Meta programs are unconscious mental filters that shape how we perceive, decide, and act. Originating from Neuro-Linguistic Programming (NLP), they influence not what we think, but how we think - structuring attention (sorting), motivation, and behavior. Meta programs can work against someone's goals or values when their habitual filters no longer match the demands of their current context or circumstances - for example, a "detail-focused" thinker may struggle to lead strategically if they can't zoom out to see the bigger picture. Similarly, a person driven by "away-from" motivation might sabotage growth opportunities by over-prioritizing risk avoidance, even when their deeper values call for bold action or connection. Now if these persons are leaders of major corporations we can see the implications of their dominant meta programs reflected in sometimes declining empires such as Kodak, Blockbuster, Sears, Nokia (US). For this reason a proper decision-making audit may be necessary from individual level to corporate and institutional environments.

As we begin to realize - Meta Programs shape perception, motivation, and decision-making; therefore any misalignment can quietly create inner conflict or repeated mistakes. Understanding meta programs - both our own and those of others - opens up doors to be remarkable flexible. Once recognized, they allow individuals to shift perspectives, reframe challenges, and choose responses that better fit the moment. By learning to flex between patterns like "towards" and "away-from" or "internal" and "external," people become remarkably adaptable, able to navigate diverse contexts with precision, empathy, and strategic clarity. In coaching, leadership, or communication, it allows us to tailor our approach to fit another person's motivational patterns rather than push against them. By recognizing these internal filters, we move from automatic reaction to conscious choice, transforming the way we relate, decide, and create results.

In our brains software we use about 50-60 of them. Here are some the most widely used ones.

Towards – Away: A person sets "toward" goals e.g., wealth, freedom, mastery - but is unconsciously motivated more by "away from" drivers e.g., avoiding failure, fear of loss. As a result, they procrastinate or self-sabotage, **since moving toward their goal doesn't feel as urgent as avoiding pain.**

Since these two are such major impactful internal programs let's dive deeper into it.

Thes patterns shows up not only in individuals but also in organizations and their management, as evidenced by once-dominant corporations that have declined or vanished.

Many of us are internally structured in a way that leads us to express, again and again, what we don't want.

In this case, the prevailing mental habit is to frame outcomes in negative terms - something that occurs automatically and, more often than not, unconsciously.

Here are some examples: I don' want to lose money; I don't want this; I don't want to have a problem; I don't want to be in an un-loving relationship; I don't want to have a boring job; I don't want to be micro-managed; I don't want to be overwhelmed; I don't want to be poor .... and so on. When we phrase it like this, we effectively reinforce this lived condition through our language. Effective change moves further away.

What are the implications for individuals who lack awareness of this internal dynamic - especially in how they communicate and how it shapes their relationships, work, and career? When the primary focus is on avoiding what they don't want, without a clearly defined direction to move toward, they tend to drift, searching for a sense of satisfaction through trial and error. They meet only the minimum criteria, guided by a perceptual filter that keeps their attention fixed on avoidance rather than intention. It filters away the focus on the positive, preventing a clearly defined outcome and the results that can be created in such a context, which would be a much more useful strategy.

By constantly avoiding what's perceived as negative we are training ourselves to become masters in this domain, always paying attention to the things we don't want. When you finally have successfully avoided what you don't want then what's left? You have no more goals unless the circumstance change so much that discomfort arises and the circle starts anew. If your aim is to be disappointed and unhappy this process is a great strategy for it. Why? It steers your focus toward the perceived negative, deepening a pessimistic mindset and coloring your internal sense of what the world is like.

Over time, this creates emotional fatigue. Avoidance requires constant vigilance, and the nervous system becomes trained to scan for threats instead of possibilities. The person begins to experience life through a narrow lens of caution and defensiveness. Their identity subtly shifts toward being reactive rather than creative, defined more by what they are trying to escape than by what they hope to build. This affects communication as well: their language becomes vague, negative, or ambiguous, making it difficult for others to understand their intentions or trust their direction.

In relationships and work, the consequences accumulate. Colleagues and partners sense the lack of clarity and feel the instability that comes from someone who cannot articulate what they want. Decisions are delayed, opportunities are missed, and conflicts repeat because the underlying pattern remains unexamined. Over the long term, this avoidance-based orientation limits growth, erodes confidence, and leads to a life organized around preventing discomfort rather than pursuing fulfillment. It is a subtle but powerful drift away from self-determination, vision, and meaningful progress.

Psychologically, this creates a sense of being carried by circumstances rather than directing them. The person begins to feel that life "happens to them".

Now - every Meta Program has its useful contextual applications - let's consider this for

Away-From can be an effective strategy for preventing negative future consequences. It's important, however, to distinguish between an ingrained, habitual Away-From mindset and a deliberate, intentional use of this approach.

When intentional we could call this also a **Strategy for Anticipation.**

Many people move through life without an internal strategy for anticipating the highly predictable elements of their future by continuing "as is". They fail to notice the patterns that consistently repeat, the outcomes that naturally follow certain choices, and situations they create, that are all a logic consequence given their current trajectory. Without this anticipatory awareness, they are left reacting to events rather than shaping them. As a result, they often find themselves facing outcomes they neither wanted nor consciously chose.

Let's use an example of financial security. At what age can I stop working without compromising my own or my family's financial needs?

Working is my choice, and I own that choice. By intentionally stepping into my future, I can set a goal and outline the steps required - right now and as the path continues to unfold. Every month, I review my plan and ask, "Am I actually on track with my savings and investments."

Other examples, a trader may exit a position immediately when clear signals indicate rising risk - avoiding a large drawdown. A manager might intervene early to prevent a small conflict from escalating into a toxic team dynamic.

In situations where danger, loss, or harm is likely, focusing on what you want to avoid creates urgency, sharpens attention, and triggers protective action. It's a survival-oriented strategy that helps people move quickly and decisively away from threats.

Options vs. Procedures:

The Options and Procedures meta programs describe two fundamentally different ways people navigate tasks and decisions. Individuals with an Options orientation prefer flexibility, alternatives, and the freedom to choose among multiple paths; they think in possibilities and adapt easily when circumstances change. Those with a Procedures orientation, by contrast, feel most effective when following a defined sequence of steps that leads to a known outcome;

they value structure, order, and proven methods. Both patterns are useful, but they shape behavior in distinct ways: Options-oriented people innovate and explore, while Procedures-oriented people execute reliably and consistently. Understanding this distinction helps explain why some individuals thrive in open-ended environments while others excel when clear instructions and established processes are in place.

A role requires following structured steps (procedures), but the person's natural preference is options, variety, and improvisation. This pattern can result in inconsistent execution, errors, or frustration with routine.

Internal vs. External Frame of Reference:

The Internal and External Frames of Reference describe how people determine whether they are on the right track. Individuals with an Internal Frame rely primarily on their own judgment, intuition, and internal standards; they know from within when something is correct or complete. We could describe the as strong self-trusting. Their decisions are guided by inner criteria, being less dependent on approval or validation from others. These individuals can act decisively under uncertainty and possess high autonomy.

Typical language patterns are:

"I just know when it's right."

"This doesn't align with my standards."

"I trust my judgment."

"It doesn't sit well with me."

Individuals who operate from this meta program often display remarkable resilience under pressure, a strong sense of identity and direction, and the ability to lead without needing consensus, maintaining clarity even amid noise or shifting market narratives. However, when this pattern is overused, it can create significant blind spots, including a tendency to ignore market feedback or resist corrective data. In these moments, their confidence may harden into rigidity, causing them to appear dismissive or closed to alternative perspectives.

In comparison, those with an External Frame look to outside sources - feedback, metrics, evaluations, or the opinions of others - to confirm whether they are doing well. Both patterns have strengths: internally referenced people are self-directed and confident in their own assessments, while externally referenced individuals excel in environments where collaboration, feedback, and external benchmarks matter. Understanding this distinction helps explain why some people trust their own sense of "rightness," while others feel most secure when validation comes from outside.

Someone who relies heavily on external validation - needs constant reassurance from colleagues before trusting your own judgment. Measuring success only by likes, sales, or praise rather than by your own standards. They can begin feeling anxious or unworthy when feedback isn't immediate or positive. To create success in their role requires trusting an internal compass (judgment, conviction). As a result, people can encounter decision paralysis, overreliance on others' opinions, and lack of confidence.

"What do others think is right?"

Typical characteristics for individuals with this meta program – they are highly responsive to feedback, and many times depend on it. They will be sensitive to standards, rules, benchmarks and seeking validation, guidance, or consensus.

Typical language patterns:

"What do you think?"

"The data says..."

"Experts agree that..."

"Let's see how this is received."

When this meta program operates in the background, it enhances alignment with reality and key stakeholders, supports strong calibration to the surrounding environment, and naturally reduces ego-driven decision-making. As a result, individuals tend to function more effectively within regulated, structured, or collaborative systems where clarity, responsiveness, and grounded judgment are essential.

When this meta program is overused, it can lead to decision paralysis, a gradual erosion of personal authority, and an unhealthy dependence on external approval. Over time, the individual becomes increasingly susceptible to trends, groupthink, and the shifting preferences of others, weakening their ability to act from internal conviction or maintain a stable sense of direction.

General vs. Specific: A trader who naturally operates from a "General" meta program excels at seeing broad market structure, identifying overarching themes, and framing trades within a larger strategic narrative. This big-picture orientation can be a real strength, especially in environments where context, regime shifts, and macro alignment matter. But when this tendency isn't balanced with enough specificity, it can create practical challenges: entries and exits become vague, risk parameters lack precision, and trade plans remain too conceptual to execute cleanly. Without translating the big idea into concrete levels, triggers, and contingencies, the trader may experience hesitation, inconsistent follow-through, or misalignment between strategy and actual trades.

A manager who operates from a predominantly "general" meta program brings valuable big-picture thinking, strategic clarity, and the ability to frame work in broad, meaningful terms. However, when this style isn't balanced with enough specificity, it can create gaps between intention and execution. Teams that rely on concrete instructions may feel unclear about priorities, unsure how to proceed, or left without the detailed steps needed for follow-through

Sameness vs. Difference: A trader with a strong sameness bias naturally gravitates toward continuity, familiar patterns, and stable routines. This can be a real asset in environments where consistency, discipline, and repeatable processes matter. However, when markets shift and the edge requires innovation or differentiation, this preference for the familiar can become a liability. The trader may cling to outdated setups, resist exploring new tools or strategies, or overlook emerging opportunities because they don't fit established templates. Over time, this creates stagnation, slower adaptation to changing conditions, and an erosion of competitive edge - especially in markets where novelty, speed of learning, and strategic evolution determine long-term survival.

In rapport building, people with a sameness orientation tend to connect through shared experiences, common values, and points of agreement. They build trust by highlighting what is familiar and stable. Those with a difference orientation, however, often engage through contrast, novelty, and distinctions. They feel energized by exploring what's new, unique, or divergent. When these styles meet, communication can either feel naturally aligned or subtly separated - one person seeking common ground while the other seeks differentiation - shaping the ease, depth, and flow of the interaction.

Proactive vs. Reactive: A trader who needs to operate proactively - planning scenarios, positioning ahead of key inflection points, and executing with intention - may still find themselves unconsciously slipping into a reactive mode. Instead of driving their strategy, they wait for perfect confirmation, rely heavily on external signals, or respond only after the market has already moved. This reactive posture creates a subtle but costly lag: opportunities appear only in hindsight, entries come late, and exits are driven by emotion rather than plan. Over time, the trader shifts from leading their strategy to chasing the market, entering trends after the edge has decayed and exiting only when discomfort peaks. The result is a pattern of missed setups, diminished expectancy, and a growing sense that the market is always one step ahead - when in reality, the trader is simply not acting from their intended proactive framework.

Convincer Strategy: A trader who naturally needs substantial evidence over time to feel convinced - what you'd call a slow convincer - can struggle in fast-moving environments that demand rapid decisions. Their internal need for repeated confirmation clashes with the market's pace, creating hesitation at critical moments. As a result, opportunities appear and disappear before they feel ready to act, leading to indecision, late entries, or missed trades altogether. Over time, this mismatch between their conviction cycle and the market's tempo can generate frustration, self-doubt, and a sense of always being a step behind, even when their analytical instincts are sound.

A **meta program misalignment** occurs when your internal "operating system" doesn't match the demands of your environment, role, or goals. When this happens, even strong abilities can feel out of sync, creating friction, inefficiency, or unnecessary strain. Developing awareness of your meta programs gives you two powerful options: you can redesign aspects of your environment to better fit your natural patterns, or you can consciously flex your internal filters and behaviors to operate more effectively. This adaptability is what restores alignment, performance, and ease.

How do we realign?

Realignment begins with identifying your dominant meta programs - your automatic filters for processing information, making decisions, and responding to the market. Journaling your reactions to trades is one of the most effective ways to surface these patterns: Do you cut winners too quickly, hesitate on entries, or get lost in excessive detail? Personality or NLP-based assessments can further clarify which filters drive your behavior. Once you understand your internal wiring, the key is to match your trading strategy to your psychology, ensuring that your methods, timeframes, and execution style align with how you naturally think and operate. This alignment restores clarity, confidence, and consistency.

Your **motivational direction** plays a major role in strategy fit, While a toward-motivated trader is often energized by opportunity and forward movement - making breakout or trend-following strategies feel intuitively appealing - this alignment isn't universal. The mindset may support the idea of riding strength, but trend-following also demands patience, comfort with repeated small losses, and the discipline to hold winners longer than feels natural. Some toward-motivated traders are actually too eager, entering prematurely or overtrading when momentum is unclear. In reality, motivational direction is just one lens among many; true strategy fit depends on a trader's risk tolerance, emotional responses, timeframe, and ability to execute under uncertainty. while an "away motivated" trader may feel more at home with mean-reversion, hedged, or risk-containment strategies. Beyond strategy selection, it's essential to adapt your environment so it supports your natural patterns - whether that means using checklists to anchor detail-oriented tasks or dashboards that help big-picture thinkers stay oriented.

Lifestyle integration matters just as much: misalignment often intensifies when fatigue, clutter, or external pressures amplify your psychological filters. Aligning your trading rhythm with your personal rhythms reduces friction and restores a sense of flow.

Values vs. Needs

Values are the guiding principles that shape who we aspire to be - like freedom, integrity, or love.

Needs are the essential conditions we require to survive and function, such as safety, connection, or rest.

Incongruence arises when honoring a value threatens to compromise a core need, or vice versa. In trading, inner conflict often arises when personal values and immediate needs pull in opposite directions.

A trader may deeply value patience, discipline, and long-term growth, yet feel a pressing need for quick results, validation, or financial security. When these forces clash, decision-making becomes strained impulsivity, may override strategy, or hesitation may replace decisive action. Over time, this tension can erode confidence and clarity, as the trader oscillates between what feels right and what seems necessary. Recognizing and reconciling this gap aligning trading behavior with both values and genuine needs, restores coherence and supports sustainable performance.

Here are some additional examples:

Valuing freedom but needing structure to thrive - often shows up in career or relationship dilemmas.

The trader deeply values integrity - following their system, honoring risk parameters, and trading only when setups meet their criteria. This reflects a commitment to long-term mastery and self-respect.

But after a series of losses or financial pressure (e.g., bills piling up, professional or family expectations), the trader feels an urgent need to generate income quickly. This need tempts them to abandon their system, force trades, or take excessive risk.

A trader may experience inner turmoil - knowing they're violating their principles while feeling justified by circumstance. This incongruence erodes confidence, clouds judgment, and often leads to deeper losses, reinforcing the cycle.

Time-based Incongruence

Time-based incongruencies occur when our past, present, and future selves are not aligned in their intentions or identities. The trader we once were may still carry fear or regret that clashes with the confident, risk-tolerant mindset we strive for today. Likewise, our envisioned future self may demand levels of mastery or freedom that the present self doesn't yet feel capable of embodying. These internal time conflicts create friction - pulling attention backward or projecting it too far ahead - making it difficult to act with coherence in the present moment. Integrating these temporal selves allows for greater consistency, emotional balance, and strategic clarity.

Time-based incongruencies arise when different versions of the self - past, present, or future - hold conflicting desires, beliefs, or identities. This split can manifest as nostalgia resisting change, **future goals clashing with current habits**, or a present self-feeling alienated from past decisions.

Past self, present self, and future self-disagree.

Example: "I used to love this, but now I dread it - yet I still plan to do it."

Example - Long-Term Vision vs. Short-Term Behavior

A trader claims to value long-term growth and strategic consistency - aiming to build wealth over years through disciplined swing trading or portfolio management. However, in practice, they frequently check charts every few minutes, chase intraday moves, and react emotionally to short-term price fluctuations.

The impact of this is incongruence between their stated time horizon and actual behavior creates stress, erodes strategic clarity, and leads to impulsive decisions that undermine their long-term goals. It's not just a mismatch in timeframes - it's a split in identity and intent.

Example - Strategy Loyalty vs. Present Doubt vs. Future Regret

Past Self: The trader spent months developing and backtesting a swing trading strategy based on clear technical setups and disciplined risk management. They believed in it, felt proud of the work, and committed to following it.

Present Self: After a string of losses and market volatility, the trader feels shaken. Doubt creeps in, and they're tempted to abandon the strategy or tweak it impulsively - questioning whether it still "works."

Future Self: Imagines looking back with regret, knowing they broke their own system under pressure and missed the compounding benefits of consistency. This self longs for stability, mastery, and the confidence that comes from honoring one's process.

Role-Based Incongruence

Role-based incongruence arises when the expectations, responsibilities, or behaviors associated with a particular role conflict with a person's authentic values or other roles they occupy. In trading, for example, a trader may feel pressure to perform aggressively to meet organizational targets, while their personal style favors caution and measured risk. This clash can create stress, reduce effectiveness, and generate a sense of internal tension. Recognizing the influence of role-based expectations allows individuals to navigate these conflicts more consciously, aligning actions with both the role and their core self.

In a broader context - roles as parent, leader, partner, or professional - conflict with one's authentic feelings, values, or identity. This tension often creates emotional strain, as the individual navigates between external duties and internal truth, leading to burnout, resentment, or a sense of fragmentation.

Social roles demand different behaviors than authentic self.

Example: "As a manager I must be firm, but I feel like a nurturer."

Belief vs. Identity

Belief versus identity incongruence occurs when a person intellectually holds a belief - such as "I am capable" or "I deserve love" - but their deeper, identity-level programming still operates from an opposing narrative. This split often reveals itself through self-sabotage, emotional resistance, or a lingering feeling of incompleteness despite consciously affirming it. Beliefs held intellectually don't match identity-level programming.

Examples:

I believe I'm worthy, but I still act like I'm not.

To take risk is necessary, but I am cautious and responsible - this can lead to avoids sizing up. Leads to miss high probability trades.

With discipline I will win in the long run - I'm intuitive and emotionally attuned. Will lead to struggles following systems, trades on impulse.

Losses are part of the process - I'm a winner - I don't lose. May lead to shame after setbacks and revenge trading.

Mastery takes time - I should be advanced now. Can lead to Impatience; abandons strategies too soon.

In deep coaching we can target this inner friction derived from conflicting identity.

Emotional vs. Logical Split

Traders operate in a landscape where every decision carry weight, and the split between emotional impulse and logical analysis can determine whether one thrives or falters.

Emotion in trading is primal. It's the rush of euphoria after a winning streak, the gut-wrenching fear during a market correction or crash, the creeping anxiety of missing out, and the seductive pull of revenge trading.

Logic, by contrast, is the trader's compass. It's the methodical application of strategy, risk management, and statistical edge. Logical traders rely on systems - whether technical indicators, macroeconomic models, or algorithmic setups - to guide their decisions.

They accept uncertainty, plan for loss, and execute with detachment. Logic doesn't eliminate emotion; it contains it.

An emotional versus intellectual split occurs when a person's feelings and rational thoughts are at odds - such as knowing something is safe yet still feeling afraid. This internal divide can create paralysis, self-doubt, or looping behaviors, as the heart and mind pull in different directions, each insisting on its own truth.

Heart says yes, head says no.

I know it's irrational, but I still feel afraid.

Trading Example - The "Missed Move" Spiral

Logical Mindset:

There will always be another setup. I trade my edge, not my FOMO.

Emotional Reaction:

I missed the breakout - I need to jump in before it runs away again.

Split Behavior:

The trader abandons their entry rules and chases price, often entering late and getting trapped in a reversal. The logic says, "wait for confirmation" but the emotion screams "don't be left behind.

Example: The "Revenge Trade" Loop

Logical Mindset:

Losses are data. I review, reset, and protect my capital.

Emotional Reaction:

I need to win it back now. I can't end the day red."

Split Behavior:

After a loss, the trader increases size or forces trades outside their plan. The logical part knows this compounds risk, but the emotional part seeks redemption and relief.

Here is another Scenario:

A trader watches a setup unfold - a textbook pattern they've studied and back tested. But they hesitate. The trade triggers and runs beautifully... without them.

Logical Mindset:

This setup had a 70%-win rate in backtesting.

The risk was well-defined and within my parameters.

I had a clear entry, stop, and target.

Emotional Reaction:

"What if I'm wrong again?"

I've had two losses today - I can't take another hit.

I feel frozen... I don't trust myself right now.

Cultural vs. Personal Truth

Cultural versus personal truth refers to the tension between the collective narratives, norms, expectations inherited from one's society or community, and the authentic inner truths that arise from lived experience, intuition, or personal evolution. This incongruence often surfaces when an individual's values, desires, or identity diverge from what their culture deems acceptable, leading to inner conflict, shame, or a quiet rebellion that seeks integration or liberation.

Internal truth clashes with inherited norms.

Example: My culture values obedience, but I crave rebellion.

Now let's observe this in a trading environment.

The trading world often glorifies hustle - early mornings, constant screen time, high-frequency action. Social media amplifies this with images of traders grinding 16-hour days, chasing volatility, and celebrating rapid gains.

Personal Truth:

A trader realizes they perform best when allowing themselves some space e.g. fewer trades, more reflection, and a slower rhythm. They thrive on journaling, ritualized prep, and emotional clarity - not adrenaline.

The Tension:

Culture says: More is better. Grind harder. Be aggressive.

Personal truth says: Less is better. I need clarity, not chaos.

Part III – Building a Trader's Identity

Most traders focus on strategies, charts, and market news, but here's the catch: if your identity isn't aligned with how you trade, you'll end up fighting yourself. When building a trader's identity you're no longer just managing behaviors under stress, you're shaping who the trader becomes in relationship to uncertainty, risk, and money. The core identity needs to be **- I am a probability operator**, not a winner or loser. I execute edge under uncertainty, and I follow process, manage exposure, and accept variance.

Consider it this way:

Habits flow from identity. If you perceive yourself as a **"disciplined risk manager"**, you'll naturally act that way in the market. If you see yourself as a **"I am risk-taker who always bounces back,"** you probably may take reckless bets - even if your system says not to.

Identity creates consistency. Systems and strategies evolve, but who you believe you are doesn't flip-flop daily. If your trading identity is solid, it keeps you steady when markets get stormy.

Identity protects against sabotage. A lot of traders blow up accounts not because they don't know enough, but because **their actions conflict with their identity**. If deep down you don't believe you're the kind of person who deserves long-term success, you'll unconsciously cut corners or overtrade.

It's like going to the gym: if you identify as someone who's "fit and healthy," and this is the point: there is no need to push yourself every day with sheer willpower - you just do the things that fit who you are. Trading works the same way.

What's important: a strong trader identity is what glues discipline, consistency, and resilience together. Without it, even the best strategy eventually collapses under emotional pressure.

"Who am I, and what identity am I choosing?"

Context shapes the answer. In trading, the real question becomes: Who do I want to be in this environment?

That level of clarity demands honest self-awareness - the ability to recognize what I do well, what's missing, and what must evolve.

As I explore these questions, I'm not just describing my current state; I'm uncovering the path from where I am to who I intend to become. That journey hinges on two anchors:

Mission: the external roadmap that guides what I'm building.

Purpose: the internal compass that directs how I show up.

Together, they define the identity I'm training toward.

What are our values? Many believe that our identity is something static, chiseled in stone, unmovable. But to the contrary - change a belief or change a habit and your identity will be different.

Designing your trader persona

Designing your trader persona means intentionally defining the qualities, habits, and mindset you want to embody every time you engage with the market. Rather than letting your trading identity form by accident - shaped by past losses, emotional reactions, or random successes - you deliberately choose the traits that align with consistent performance, such as patience, adaptability, and strategic thinking. This persona becomes a mental "uniform" you step into before each trading session, influencing how you respond to uncertainty, manage risk, and interpret market signals. By visualizing and rehearsing this ideal version of yourself, you program your mind to trade in alignment with your chosen identity, making disciplined action feel natural rather than forced.

Discipline

The Roots of Discipline are our Internal Belief Systems

Belief systems are the silent foundation of behavior. They shape how we interpret risk, respond to setbacks, and define success. When these internal narratives are unconscious or fragmented, discipline becomes brittle - easily disrupted by stress, temptation, or ambiguity. But when belief systems are consciously examined and refined, they become a source of strength. For example:

A trader who believes "I am only valuable when I win" may chase volatility and burn out.

A reframed belief - "I am valuable when I act with integrity and clarity" - supports steadier decision-making and emotional resilience.

This reframing isn't cosmetic. It's archetypal. It invites the individual to shift from reactive scripts to intentional identities - The Steward, The Strategist, The Alchemist - each carrying its own rituals, boundaries, and ethical compass.

Internal Alignment, Discipline, Willpower

How many of you associate discipline as an act of willpower or something which is levied on you from an outside force under the threat of negative consequences or punishment when not exercised? This can be useful in certain contexts. Do we mistake discipline for obedience - something enforced by fear rather than chosen from clarity.

If we spin this further, the use of willpower can be an indicator that internal incongruencies are present. What do I mean by that?

Let's practice a reframe with the notion of discipline and common associations attached to it, this is after all a book about the practice and implementation of Neurolinguistic Programming.

"Discipline is cool"

Companion of Freedom

Discipline, you walk with me,

Not as a cage, but liberty.

A trusted guide through dusk and dawn,

A melody I've always drawn.

With every choice, with every hour,

You turn my will into power.

What could "cool" discipline look like in your life?

Imagine **Discipline as something stylish, magnetic, and deeply desirable**, a foundation for confidence and not something I must do, have to do, but rather something I choose and aspire to. You are honoring your own word and values with consistency.

When you're clear about what you want and who you're becoming, your attention, decisions, and behavior naturally organize around that identity. The surrounding noise drops, internal friction dissolves, and your actions line up with your intentions. As a result, alignment, congruence, and focus stop being things you chase and instead become the natural byproducts of a coherent direction.

Most of us have some form of discipline, but it's usually fragmented – perhaps stronger in certain areas, absent in others. What we call "discipline" is often just habit, fear, or obligation. Real discipline appears when identity, intention, and behavior point in the same direction.. Let's put this now into the context of trading and fine tune your approach. Where in your trading routine do you notice patterns of inconsistency or emotional override, where could you use more intentional structure or emotional congruence?

Discipline in Trading

Execution discipline in trading reveals itself precisely at the moments when emotion tries to pull you off your plan. It's the trader who takes the planned entry instead of waiting for "one more confirmation," the one who follows their stop-loss rules - whether that means holding the original level or adjusting it according to a predefined plan - rather than shifting it because the chart "might turn." It's the trader who sizes positions based on the plan instead of their confidence that day, and the one who stays out when their setup isn't present, even if the market is moving without them. In each case, discipline isn't willpower; it's the expression of a clear framework that removes negotiation and makes consistent execution a natural extension of a well-defined trading identity.

Sticking to pre-planned entry and exit rules, avoiding impulsive trades.

Using limit orders instead of chasing price movements recklessly.

Avoiding overtrading - recognizing when the market isn't providing quality setups.

Waiting for a confirmed breakout above a resistance level with volume exceeding 1.5x average before entering.

Sets a x% volatility adjusted stop-loss and honoring it without moving it mid-trade.

Risk Management Discipline is the integration of a trader's psychology with a clear technical framework. The psychological side is the ability to tolerate uncertainty, accept small losses, and resist the urge to override rules when emotions spike. The technical side is the structure that makes consistency possible: position-sizing formulas, predefined invalidation levels, volatility-based stops, and limits that prevent impulsive decisions. Discipline shows up when the trader follows these rules in real time, especially when the market tempts them to improvise. When psychology and process work together, risk management becomes less about restriction and more about protecting the conditions that allow your edge to play out.

Maintaining consistent position sizing, regardless of emotions or recent wins/losses.

Never risking more than a set percentage (e.g., 1-2% of capital per trade).

Adjusting stop losses based on market volatility, not fear.

Daily and monthly loss limits.

Psychological & Emotional Discipline is the ability to stay grounded when your internal state wants to pull you off course. It's the capacity to feel fear, excitement, frustration, or urgency without letting those emotions dictate your decisions. A key part of this is recognizing cognitive biases - like confirmation bias, where you instinctively favor information that supports your existing beliefs - and catching them before they distort your perception of the market. It also involves using mindfulness techniques to reduce emotional interference, creating just enough mental space to respond deliberately rather than react impulsively. In that space, discipline isn't suppression; it's self-leadership that keeps your actions aligned with who you intend to be.

Strategy Discipline keeps you from chasing noise, over-adapting to short-term outcomes, or abandoning your process after a streak of wins or losses. Psychologically, it's the ability to tolerate uncertainty without rewriting your rules, and to trust the long-term expectancy of your edge even when the short-term results are uncomfortable

Sticking to tested trading setups rather than constantly switching strategies.

Avoiding trades outside of your expertise (e.g., a swing trader suddenly scalping).

Adapting but not abandoning core principles during market shifts.

Executes trades that match their defined setup (e.g. trend continuation with pullback to 20 EMA).

Strategy-Specific Risk Allocation e.g., allocating more risk to high-probability set-ups, less to experimental ones - but always within predefined limits.

No Strategy Stacking e.g., avoiding combining multiple strategies in one trade (e.g., breakout + mean reversion).

Strategy Review Ritual e.g., Monthly review of strategy performance metrics: win rate, expectancy, drawdown.

Time & Routine Discipline is the commitment to show up consistently and follow a structured daily process rather than reacting to the market's noise. It means preparing the same way each day - reviewing levels, assessing conditions, and aligning your mindset before making decisions. A stable routine becomes an anchor that reduces randomness, sharpens focus, and keeps your actions intentional.

Following a structured pre-market routine, including research and scenario planning.

Managing screen time - knowing when to step away instead of forcing trades.

Reviewing performance regularly to improve weaknesses.

Top traders integrate these forms into a holistic framework, balancing technical execution with psychological resilience.

Focus as Discipline - The Art of Intentional Attention

In an environment built to pull your attention away, focus has to be practiced intentionally. The quiet art of choosing what matters and defending it against the irrelevant and the noise. Focused attention arises naturally when your internal mindset and external surroundings support each other. At the core lies clarity of intention. Knowing exactly what you are focusing on - and why - gives attention direction and purpose. When goals are vague or competing, attention fragments and effort becomes scattered. Alongside clarity, motivation and emotion play a crucial role. The level of interest, the meaning given, or emotional investment strengthen focus, while boredom, stress, or indifference weaken focus. Cognitive energy is the mental fuel that sustains attention. Fatigue, multitasking, and overstimulation quickly drain this resource. Equally, the environment shapes our ability to stay attentive: calm, structured surroundings support concentration, whereas noise and constant interruptions erode it.

We can protect our time and energy by setting boundaries.

When prioritizing wisely we choose what truly matters and letting go of the rest – it doesn't need to be completed now and does not need occupy our mental space. We just put it into existence and at a time of our choosing we can re-engage. It could be taken even a step further by viewing choosing itself as a deliberate practice of self-awareness.

The Importance of Creating Well-Formed Goals and Outcomes

Creating a Goal vs. Creating an Outcome

A goal is a direction. An outcome is a result. Most traders blur the two, which is why their intentions feel vague and their progress feels inconsistent. A goal gives you something to aim at; an outcome gives you something to measure. Both matter, but they serve different psychological functions.

Creating well-formed outcomes is one of the most powerful ways to bring clarity, direction, and momentum into any change process. Vague intentions like "I want to improve" or "I should be more disciplined" rarely lead to meaningful results because they lack structure. A well-formed goal, by contrast, transforms desire into a precise map. It defines *what* you want, *why* it matters, and *how* you will know you're on the right track (Evidence Frame).

The process forces you to move from being abstract to being specific. When a goal is concrete, measurable, and grounded in your own control, it becomes actionable. You shift from reacting to circumstances to proactively shaping them. Well-formed goals also reveal hidden obstacles, internal doubts, misaligned values, or competing commitments - so you can address them before they derail progress.

Equally important is the emotional resonance behind the outcome. When a goal is framed in sensory-rich detail, aligned with your values, and imagined as already achieved, it becomes far more motivating. The mind begins to operate with a clear picture of success, activating resourceful states and improving decision quality.

In short, well-formed goals don't simply organize your intentions; they upgrade your behavior. They become the basis for alignment between belief, strategy, and action, making it much easier for the nervous system to commit, persist, and adapt. With a well-formed outcome, you're no longer hoping for change - you're guiding it with precision and purpose.

Last but not least – you want to use the "towards" metaprogram and not "away"! Too often I find in my work that people tell you what they don't want. Be aware that you are not using "away" as part of your operating system unless specifically needed.

The Outcome Frame: A Blueprint for Effective Change

The Outcome Frame is a core NLP tool designed to clarify goals and create the conditions for successful change moving beyond stating what you don't want and instead focuses on what you do want, ensuring outcomes are specific, contextual, actionable, and expressed in positive terms. It shifts thinking from problem-centered to solution-oriented, providing a mental map that guides both strategy and behavior. At its essence, the Outcome Frame asks a series of structured questions: What exactly do you want? How will you know when you have it? What resources, skills, or behaviors are needed? What will achieving this outcome give you, and what might you risk or lose? By systematically addressing these questions, this frame ensures the goal is well-formed, grounded in reality, and aligned with your values and identity.

Using the Outcome Frame brings multiple benefits. It reduces ambiguity, highlights potential obstacles, and identifies missing resources, making it easier to plan effective steps toward the desired result. It also strengthens motivation by connecting the outcome to personally meaningful reasons for change. Importantly, it provides a feedback loop: knowing how to recognize success keeps the mind engaged and responsive, rather than wandering or defaulting to old patterns.

In short, the Outcome Frame transforms goals from abstract wishes into precise, actionable targets. It aligns attention, behavior, and internal resources, creating a structured path that turns intention into tangible results. By framing change in this way, achieving meaningful outcomes becomes not just possible, but inevitable.

Generative Coaching - Guiding Those Who Don't Know What They Want

Generative coaching is a transformative approach designed not just to overcome obstacles, but to help individuals create new possibilities for their lives. For someone who doesn't yet know what they want, it provides a structured yet creative space to explore, uncover, and generate clarity without pressure or judgment. Instead of starting with a predefined goal, the process begins by understanding the person's values, strengths, patterns, and the life they naturally aspire to lead.

At the heart of generative coaching is the idea that people already carry the seeds of their next evolution within them - hidden in intuition, past experiences, or embodied knowing. The coach's role is to ask generative questions, guide awareness, and create experiments in thought and physical expression that reveal these possibilities. This might involve exploring identity, imagining future scenarios, noticing recurring patterns, or trying small shifts in thought or behavior to see what resonates. Over time, these explorations crystallize into a clearer sense of purpose and direction.

For someone uncertain about their desires, this approach is especially powerful because it reduces the anxiety of having to "figure it out" immediately. Instead, it emphasizes curiosity, creativity, and alignment. By connecting what emerges to the individual's values, energy, and natural inclinations, generative coaching moves them from confusion to confidence, turning the unknown into actionable, meaningful outcomes.

In essence, generative coaching cultivates the conditions for clarity to arise. It transforms uncertainty into opportunity, allowing people to discover not just what they want, but who they are capable of becoming.

"It's never too late to become the person you could have been"

T. Elliot

Define the Trader You Want to Be – From Present State to Desired State

Instead of focusing only on outcomes such - as "I want to make X% a year in a defined strategy with a maximum drawdown of/or % capital at risk" - describe your identity.

Ask yourself: "What is my identity as a trader" - Then test how it resonates for you?

Do I want to be - a calculating risk manager - an adaptive strategist - a disciplined executor?

Make certain you are using well-formed language "I am a trader who..."

Don't' use "I want to be a trader..."

Now there will be obstacles in this process. One way to overcome them will be using an "As If" frame.

The Usefulness of "As If Frames" for Outcome Generation

"As If Frames" are one of the most elegant mental tools for generating outcomes because they bypass resistance and invite the mind to operate from possibility rather than limitation. Instead of asking "Can I do this?" - a question that often triggers doubt - you step into the scenario as if the desired outcome were already true. This temporary suspension of disbelief gives the nervous system a different set of references: confidence instead of hesitation, creativity instead of constraint, and solutions instead of problems.

By imagining yourself acting, deciding, and responding from the version of you who has already achieved the goal, you activate new behavioral options. The frame shifts attention away from current obstacles and toward the strategies, attitudes, and micro-behaviors that would naturally align with the outcome. It becomes easier to identify what needs to change because you're no longer analyzing from today's limitations - you're mapping from tomorrow's competence.

In outcome generation, "As If Frames" also reduce emotional friction. When people think as if the outcome is already real, motivation often rises, internal conflicts soften, and clarity sharpens. It becomes less about forcing change and more about embodying a trajectory. The frame essentially unlocks a rehearsal space in the mind where future success can be practiced, refined, and felt -turning distant goals into tangible possibilities.

The Relevancy Procedure and Identifying the Missing Link

The relevancy procedure is a powerful NLP method that helps uncover *why* a desired change isn't happening, even when the goal is clear and motivation seems present. It works by examining the connection - or lack of connection - between the outcome a person wants and the internal structures that drive their behavior: beliefs, values, identity, and emotional payoffs. When these deeper layers don't recognize the goal as relevant, the nervous system simply won't mobilize toward it.

At the heart of the procedure is the search for the *missing link* - the specific element that prevents the goal from becoming meaningful or actionable. This missing link might be an unacknowledged fear, a conflicting belief, a value mismatch, or a secondary gain that makes the current situation feel safer than change. Identifying it brings clarity to why progress feels blocked despite best intentions.

Once the missing link is revealed, the goal can be reframed so it becomes personally important at a deeper level. The mind begins to perceive the outcome not as an abstract desire but as something that fits naturally into the person's identity, values, and lived experience. This shifts the internal system from hesitation to alignment.

The relevancy procedure therefore transforms goals from "something I should do" into "something that matters to who I am." When the missing link is found and integrated, resistance dissolves, clarity strengthens, and forward movement becomes far more fluid and sustainable.

Possibilities for a new Trader Identity

When forming a new trader identity, confusion can arise because multiple roles overlap without being clearly differentiated. A trader may operate as a strategist and adaptive trader, generating ideas and adjusting to changing conditions, yet lack the disciplined executor who reliably acts within predefined constraints. Others develop strong risk management frameworks but miss the risk operator identity that enacts those rules moment by moment under pressure. A mature trader identity emerges when these roles are consciously separated and then integrated, allowing each to appear at the right time rather than competing for control.

Step mentally into these frames and perceive how they align with you. Do some dry runs and be creative! You will evolve over time, and these roles can become more flexible and weave into each other. Begin identifying the core qualities required for this identity and deliberately observe the behaviors that must accompany them. What's already there – what's missing, what do I want to improve and put my full intention behind it. Allow yourself to fully experience this declaration somatically as well.

The Risk Manager

In trading, risk is not managed after decisions - it is managed continuously as part of the decision itself."

The Risk Manager/Operator is a trader who prioritizes the preservation of capital and the control of exposure above all else. They systematically identify, assess, and mitigate potential threats, using disciplined frameworks to balance opportunity with safety. By keeping emotions in check and adhering to clear risk parameters, they ensure resilience and sustainability in volatile markets. What are the characteristics an excellent risk manager possess?

A good Risk Manager/Operator combines clear perception with disciplined action. At the core is the ability to distinguish uncertainty from danger (probability of loss beyond acceptable limits) - to recognize that not all unknowns are threats, yet some threats demand decisive limits. This requires emotional regulation: staying calm under pressure, resisting impulsive reactions, and avoiding both fear-driven paralysis and overconfident exposure.

Sound judgment is another essential quality. A strong risk manager thinks in probabilities rather than certainties, weighs asymmetric outcomes, and consistently asks, "What happens if I'm wrong?" They focus less on predicting outcomes and more on controlling downside, preserving optionality, and surviving adverse scenarios.

Equally important is self-awareness. Effective risk operator understand their own cognitive and emotional biases - loss aversion, confirmation bias, recency effects - and actively design rules and processes to neutralize them. This includes predefined limits, clear exit criteria, and a willingness to cut losses without self-justification.

Finally, a good Risk Manager/Operator is both humble and consistent. Humility keeps them open to new information and respectful of randomness; consistency ensures that principles are applied regardless of mood or recent results. Together, these qualities create a mindset that prioritizes longevity over short-term wins - recognizing that sustainable success is not built on avoiding risk, but on engaging it intelligently and deliberately.

Ultimately the risk manager decides how much risk is appropriate, when to scale, and when to step back.

You can anchor that with a motto or slogan: "Defense creates offense."

The Strategist

The Strategist is a trader who approaches the market with foresight and careful planning, analyzing patterns, probabilities, and potential outcomes before taking action. They balance risk and opportunity, crafting adaptable plans that anticipate change rather than simply reacting to it. Their edge comes from thoughtful preparation, scenario thinking, and a measured approach to decision-making.

Strategic thinking requires the ability to integrate multiple levels at once: vision and execution, present conditions and future implications, internal capabilities and external realities. A strong strategist understands leverage - where a small, well-placed decision can create disproportionate impact - and allocates attention and resources accordingly.

Focus: Big-picture, market structure, patient setups.

Sees beyond individual trades, focusing on the bigger picture (portfolio context, long-term performance, and market cycles).

Pattern Recognition & Market Insight

Probabilistic Mindset - Thinks in probabilities, not certainties.

Frames each trade as a distribution of outcomes, rather than a binary win/loss.

Accepts uncertainty as a constant and avoids overconfidence.

Recognizes recurring market structures, behaviors, and anomalies. Understands the interaction between macroeconomic forces, sentiment, liquidity, and technical signals.

Uses both quantitative data and intuitive sense developed through experience.

Frames trades within a coherent decision framework, not isolated hunches.

Develops clear objectives: capital preservation, alpha generation, or risk-adjusted returns.

Motto: "Wait, then strike."

The Adaptive Trader

The Adaptive Trader is someone who navigates markets with flexibility, responding to changing conditions rather than rigid rules. They integrate self-awareness, emotional regulation, and strategic thinking to adjust their approach in real time. By balancing intuition with analysis, they learn from both successes and setbacks, continuously evolving their methods to maintain resilience and consistency.

Their flexibility is disciplined: they refine position sizing as volatility expands, tighten risk when clarity fades, or shift tactics within the limits of their established playbook. Every adjustment has a reason, a purpose, and a place within their identity as a trader. Adaptation strengthens their edge because it is deliberate, documented, and aligned with long-term consistency.

What about Style drift you may ask. Style drift by contrast, is change without structure. It emerges when a trader abandons their plan in response to discomfort - after a losing streak, a missed move, or the emotional pull of FOMO. Instead of adjusting parameters within their strategy, they leap to entirely different methods, timeframes, or instruments, often without realizing it. These shifts are reactive, unmeasured, and driven by short-term P/L rather than market structure. Over time, style drift erodes identity, obscures performance data, and dissolves any chance of building a repeatable edge.

The difference is simple but profound: adaptation is intentional evolution; style drift is emotional escape. One builds a resilient trader who can thrive across regimes. The other fragments the process and undermines long-term success. Understanding this divide is essential for any trader seeking mastery in a world defined by uncertainty.

Motto: "Change is my edge."

The Disciplined Executor

is the trader who transforms intention into consistent action. They operate from a well-defined plan and treat that plan as the anchor of their decision-making, especially when markets become noisy or emotionally charged. Instead of reacting to every fluctuation, they follow a structured process that tells them when to enter, when to exit, how much to risk, and when to stand aside. Their discipline is not rigidness - it's clarity. They know exactly what qualifies as a valid opportunity and what does not, which frees them from the constant negotiation that derails less structured traders.

What sets the Disciplined Executor apart is their commitment to long-term objectives. They understand that edge plays out over sequences, not single trades, and they refuse to let short-term emotions distort their behavior. Their routines - pre-market preparation, journaling, risk checks, execution reviews - create a stable rhythm that keeps them grounded regardless of market conditions. When volatility spikes, they don't abandon their plan; they tighten their process. When boredom creeps in, they don't force trades; they return to their criteria. Their emotional management is proactive, not reactive.

Motto: "Process over outcome."

Some others to consider -The Steward of Capital - The Probability Professional - The Risk Executor - The Market Operator - The Portfolio Operator

The power of creating mottos lies in their ability to distill complex intentions, values, or strategies into a simple, memorable phrase that guides thought and action. A well-crafted motto acts as a mental anchor, providing clarity in moments of uncertainty and reinforcing consistency in behavior. By repeatedly invoking it, individuals can strengthen focus, maintain alignment with their goals, and cultivate the mindset needed to navigate challenges with purpose. Be creative and find a motto that fits you.

Moving from a present state to a desired state begins with clarity: clearly defining the goal and understanding the gap between where you are and where you want to be. Next comes assessment and planning, identifying resources, obstacles, and actionable steps needed to bridge that gap. Execution involves consistently taking those steps while monitoring progress, adapting strategies as needed. Finally, integration and reflection ensure the new state becomes sustainable, reinforcing learning and alignment with values.

Future Pacing

Before finalizing and implementing this new identity let's future pace it. Vividly imagine yourself having already achieved a desired outcome, mentally rehearsing how you think, feel, and act in that future state. This process helps create a sense of certainty and alignment, strengthening motivation and guiding present actions toward that goal. By repeatedly envisioning success, it bridges the gap between intention and behavior. But you also want to be certain what are the consequences, intended or unintended, of the behaviors of this new or altered you.

Creating an Intention

Intention is a conscious commitment to a desired state, outcome, or way of being - it's the inner compass that guides action with purpose. Unlike fleeting goals, (you may be familiar with new year's resolutions which are not realized), or reactive impulses - intention anchors behavior in meaning, aligning thoughts, emotions, and choices toward a coherent direction. In trading, intention transforms each decision from a gamble into a deliberate expression of strategy, self-awareness, and growth.

Reflect on Your Goals: What do you want to achieve, experience, or embody? Think deeply about what matters most to you.

Choose Empowering Words: Frame your intention positively. Instead of "I don't want to fail," you can say "I am a someone who embraces learning and growth."

Keep it Simple: Focus on one intention at a time to avoid feeling overwhelmed.

Feel the Connection: Imagine how fulfilling it will be to manifest this intention and let that feeling drive you.

Take Action: Align your daily choices and habits with your intention to ensure it's more than just words.

I approach challenges with curiosity and courage," or "I prioritize my well-being by setting healthy boundaries." "I am a successful trader".

Understand Market Trends: Recognize whether the market is bullish, bearish, or neutral. Tailor your strategies, accordingly, buy pullbacks in bullish markets, short in bearish markets, and use range-bound strategies in neutral markets.

Stay Flexible: Adapt your trading strategies to changing conditions. Use tools like conditional orders and algorithmic trading to enhance responsiveness in volatile markets.

Risk Management: Protect your capital by setting stop-loss and trailing stop orders. Adjust your risk tolerance based on market volatility.

Continuous Learning: Stay informed about economic indicators, geopolitical events, and market news. Reflect on past trades to improve decision-making

Diversify Strategies: Employ a mix of trading approaches, such as hedging, portfolio adjustments, and capitalizing on emerging trends

Emotional Discipline: Avoid impulsive decisions by maintaining a calm and focused mindset. Emotional intelligence is crucial for resilience in trading.

Align Habits matching your created Identity

A habit is a thread, spun quiet in the dark -

a whisper of intention that becomes a woven mark.

At first it barely holds, a flicker, not a flame,

but stitch by daily stitch it learns to speak your name.

And when you try to change, to cut or twist or mend,

you find the thread runs deeper than you thought it ends.

Identity and habits are deeply intertwined, forming a feedback loop that shapes both behavior and self-perception. Our identity can be thought of as the collection of beliefs, values, and narratives we hold about who we are and what we are capable of. Habits, in turn, are the repeated actions and routines that emerge from, and reinforce, these beliefs. When a person consistently acts in ways aligned with a particular self-concept, those behaviors signal to the brain and to the self that the identity is real and reliable. For example, someone who identifies as disciplined will naturally engage in habits such as planning, tracking progress, and maintaining routines, which continually affirm the identity of being disciplined. Conversely, habits can also subtly shape identity over time: by adopting consistent behaviors, even without initially believing in a certain trait, a person can begin to internalize the corresponding identity. This is why small, repeated actions are so powerful - they communicate to the subconscious mind,

"This is who I am," gradually transforming self-perception and internalized values. The reinforcement is not merely psychological; it is physiological as well. Neural pathways strengthen with repetition, and the brain begins to favor patterns that align with the reinforced identity. This is particularly evident in areas like trading, sports, or creative work, where performance and resilience are intimately tied to the habits that embody one's self-concept.

Habits act as both mirrors and architects of identity: they reflect who we currently see ourselves as, and they simultaneously construct the foundation for who we can become. Awareness of this dynamic allows individuals to consciously design behaviors that cultivate desired traits, align with personal values, and create lasting change, transforming identity from a static narrative into a living, evolving system reinforced by action.

If a trader's identity is "I am disciplined," their pre-market actions reflect structure and consistency. They review their trading plan, set risk limits, study overnight market developments, and rehearse potential scenarios. They follow routines - like journaling, workspace organization, and grounding exercises - to maintain focus and emotional control. These habits reinforce the identity, turning discipline into a self-sustaining pattern of behavior.

If a trader's identity is "I am adaptive," their pre-market actions focus on flexibility and responsiveness. They scan the market for changing conditions, consider multiple strategies, and remain open to adjusting positions as new information emerges. Rather than rigid routines, they prepare to pivot quickly, maintain situational awareness, and stay mentally fluid, letting adaptability guide their decisions throughout the day.

Each small act is a vote for your trader identity.

Language and Identity

Our language is a mirror of our identity, reflecting the beliefs, values, and roles we hold about ourselves. The words and phrases we consistently use reveal how we perceive our capabilities, priorities, and place in the world. Over time, this language not only communicates identity to others but also reinforces it internally, creating a feedback loop where thought, speech, and self-concept continuously shape one another.

"Identity becomes real when habits reinforce it."

From Strategy Follower to Strategic Thinker

Most people execute strategies designed by others - they follow rules, systems, or market signals. The shift to becoming a strategic thinker begins when you stop asking "What should I do" and start asking "Why does this work or not" It's the movement from imitation to insight, from reacting to creating - where strategy becomes an expression of your own understanding, not someone else's blueprint.

Shifting from strategy follower to strategic thinker initiates a profound identity-level transformation. It redefines the self from executor to architect - someone who not only acts but anticipates, designs, and aligns with deeper patterns. This shift cultivates creative responsibility, foresight, and congruence, inviting the individual to embody a role that is generative rather than reactive, visionary rather than compliant.

Identity-level change in NLP

In NLP, identity-level change addresses the deepest layer of personal transformation - shifting how you perceive yourself, not just what you do. For traders, this means moving beyond "I use a trading strategy" to "I am a disciplined, process-driven trader." When your identity is in harmony with the behaviors you want to embody, adhering to rules, controlling risk, and learning from setbacks flow naturally as expressions of who you are, rather than as imposed routines. Without this shift, traders may cling to old patterns, sabotaging progress even when they know better. By consciously redefining identity through language, visualization, and consistent action, traders embed success-oriented behaviors at the core of their self-image, creating lasting change that persists even under market pressure.

Breaking limiting belief loops

Challenging beliefs such as "I'm not disciplined enough" begins with seeing them as constructed stories. These phrases often signal an identity freeze rather than an accurate reflection of current behavior - a conclusion drawn from moments of inconsistency rather than an accurate description of one's capacity. To break the loop, **shift the focus from**

judgment to process: instead of measuring who you are, observe what you are practicing. Discipline is not a trait you either have or lack; it's a muscle built through small, repeated acts of alignment with what truly matters to you. Each moment of follow-through, no matter how small, weakens the old identity and reinforces a new one: "I am someone who keeps promises to myself."

Self-defeating loops like "I'm just unlucky" or "I'm not disciplined enough" act as mental traps that reinforce poor trading behavior. Each time a trade goes wrong, these beliefs are reactivated, shaping perception so that failures feel inevitable and successes are dismissed as flukes. This cycle erodes confidence and reduces motivation to improve, because the trader's identity becomes fused with limitation. NLP breaks these loops by challenging the language and evidence supporting them, reframing setbacks as specific, solvable issues rather than proof of personal inadequacy. Through techniques like submodality shifts, anchoring past successes, and installing empowering self-statements, traders can replace these limiting loops with narratives that fuel resilience, skill growth, and consistent execution.

Installing a Cause–Effect Relationship from Present to Future

We humans are meaning-making creatures. We don't just experience reality; we link events, emotions, and actions through cause-and-effect relationships. These links create coherence in our story - they explain why things happen and give us a sense of direction. Yet most people unconsciously install cause–effect chains that trap them in the past .

A powerful way to deal with these limiting beliefs is to consciously install a cause–effect bridge from the present into the future - one that generates momentum, identity, and choice instead.

Here are some examples:

Limiting: Because I lost money before, I don't trust my judgment now.

Empowering: Because I'm refining my process today, I'll trust my judgment more with every decision going forward.

Limiting: Because I was criticized in the past, I hold back my ideas today.

Empowering: Because I'm expressing myself authentically today, I'll attract better collaboration tomorrow.

Limiting: Because I made mistakes before, I'm afraid to take risks now.

Empowering: Because I'm learning from each step today, I'll take smarter, more confident risks tomorrow.

Moving from Reactivity to Generative Causation

Traditional cause–effect thinking is inherently reactive because it anchors present behavior in past events rather than future intentions. It explains "why things are" instead of shaping "what could be." When cause is located behind us, our choices become justifications - not creations. **This backward orientation keeps identity and performance tied to memory, not possibility**. To move from reaction to creation, the causal link must shift from past-to-present toward present-to-future: "Because I act with clarity today, I create the conditions for excellence tomorrow."

Traditional cause–effect thinking is reactive. It says, "Because of my circumstances, I feel this way." Generative cause–effect thinking reverses this: "Because I choose to align my actions with my future vision, I am creating new circumstances."

In other words, we move from being the effect of external events **to being the cause of future outcomes**. The present moment becomes a causal point - a place of ownership, not consequence.

The Mechanics of Installation

Installing a cause–effect relationship from present to future begins with language and attention. The nervous system follows the structure of language. When we say, "Because I am focusing on what matters today, I will experience competence and peace of mind tomorrow," we establish a causal pathway that recruits both the cognitive and emotional systems toward alignment.

"By committing to disciplined consistency today - showing up, executing my process, and correcting small errors - I'm laying the structural foundations that make stability not a matter of luck, but a resulting outcome. My future results will be the compounded effect of the micro-behaviors I'm shaping now."

Define the desired future state.

Describe the specific emotional, behavioral, or situational outcome you want to experience - e.g. calm consistency in trading, creative flow, or confidence under pressure.

Anchor the present as the cause and source of change.

Link today's attitudes and actions as the generating environment. For example:

"Because I am practicing awareness in each trade today, I am building a pattern of trust in my process."

Embody the future now!

Bring the emotional tone of that desired future into the present. This creates a neuro-associative feedback loop that reinforces the cause–effect linkage at a subconscious level.

Repeat and reinforce linguistically!

Every repetition of this structure - "Because I do X now, Y will unfold" - strengthens the neural pathway. Over time, the brain learns to experience agency as natural rather than effortful.

Why It Works

The mind seeks coherence. When we consistently assert a cause–effect relationship, it fills in the evidence to make it true. By assigning causality to conscious actions in the present, we train perception and behavior to align with our intended future. The future becomes not a hope, but a logical consequence of who we are being right now.

From Possibility to Predictability

When you begin to experience the present as the cause of your future, transformation accelerates. Identity shifts. You no longer chase results - you embody the processes that make them inevitable.

The key insight is simple yet profound: Your future self is not waiting for you to arrive - it is being constructed by every causal link you install in the present.

Values Alignment in Trading

Detecting when your goals conflict with your core values

When trading goals clash with your core values, progress becomes an uphill battle marked by hidden resistance. For example, a trader who **values stability** but sets an aggressive daily profit target may unconsciously avoid taking valid setups to minimize stress, sabotaging their own performance.

Similarly, someone who values freedom might resent the structured routines necessary for consistent execution, leading to inconsistent habits. NLP helps traders uncover these conflicts by exploring the deeper "why" behind their goals and asking whether those aims truly align with their personal values. Once identified, goals can be reframed or adjusted so that pursuing them feels energizing rather than draining, creating a sustainable path to success.

Avoiding the trap of chasing profits over process

Chasing profits over process is one of the fastest ways for traders to lose consistency and discipline. When the primary focus is on making money every trade or every day, decisions tend to be driven by urgency, fear of missing out, and the need for instant validation. This mindset often leads to overtrading, abandoning strategies, and taking on excessive risk.

In contrast, process-focused traders measure success by how well they executed their plan, regardless of the outcome of any single trade. By shifting attention from short-term gains to long-term skill mastery, traders create the mental space to follow rules, adapt intelligently to market conditions, and allow their edge to play out over time - ironically leading to more consistent profits.

Designing a purpose-driven trading plan

A purpose-driven trading plan goes beyond entry and exit rules - it aligns your trading activities with your deeper motivations and life goals. Instead of trading solely for income or excitement, you define the personal "why" that makes the effort meaningful, whether it's financial independence, time freedom, intellectual challenge, or building a legacy. This clarity provides a stable foundation for decision-making, helping you stay focused during drawdowns and avoid being swayed by short-term emotions. A purpose-driven plan integrates strategy, risk management, and self-management practices, ensuring that every trade you take supports both your financial objectives and your core values. When purpose drives the plan, consistency and resilience follow naturally.

Belief Change Techniques

Belief change begins by making the invisible visible – we start identifying our unconscious assumptions that shape perception and behavior. Techniques from NLP, Gestalt, and Generative Coaching help you question these inner constructs, reframe limiting meanings, and install more empowering perspectives, therefore transforming not just what you think, but how you experience reality.

Submodalities for transforming limiting beliefs

In NLP, submodalities are the fine details of how we mentally represent experiences - such as the brightness, size, distance, sound, or texture of an internal image or memory - and they hold the key to reshaping limiting beliefs. For traders, a belief like "I can't handle large positions" might be tied to a vivid mental replay of a past loss, seen up close, in high color, and with a sinking feeling in the body. By consciously altering these submodalities -shrinking the image, fading the colors, pushing it farther away, or changing its sound - you can reduce the emotional intensity and break the belief's grip. Once the limiting representation is weakened, you can install an empowering alternative, vividly encoded with positive submodalities, to reinforce confidence and possibility in your trading mindset.

Installing beliefs of patience, resilience, and adaptability

Installing beliefs of patience, resilience, and adaptability gives traders the psychological foundation to thrive in any market environment. In NLP, beliefs are strengthened by consistent mental rehearsal, emotional anchoring, and evidence gathering. For example, a trader can vividly imagine themselves calmly waiting for the perfect setup, recall moments they recovered from setbacks, and reframe past market shifts as opportunities they adapted to successfully. By repeatedly associating these mental images and feelings with their identity as a trader, the mind begins to treat these qualities as natural and automatic. Over time, patience tempers impulsive entries, resilience transforms losses into lessons, and adaptability turns changing market conditions into a competitive advantage.

Part IV– Core NLP Principles for Traders

Key NLP presuppositions

NLP is built on a set of presuppositions - guiding beliefs that shape how we think, feel, and act - which can be especially powerful for traders. For example, "The map is not the territory" reminds **traders that their analysis is only a model of the market, not the market itself**, encouraging flexibility when conditions change. "There is nothing such as failure, only feedback" reframes losing trades as valuable data for improvement rather than personal defeat. "People have all the resources they need" reinforces the idea that discipline, patience, and adaptability can be developed through practice, rather than being fixed traits. It's not a matter of if I get there, but how I get there!

Adopting these presuppositions shifts a trader's mindset from rigid and reactive to adaptive and resourceful - qualities essential for consistent success in the unpredictable world of markets.

Representational systems (visual, auditory, kinesthetic) in trading perception

In NLP, representational systems refer to the ways people process and store information - primarily through visual, auditory, and kinesthetic channels - and these modes shape how traders perceive and interact with the markets. A visually dominant trader may focus heavily on charts, patterns, and color-coded indicators, making them highly sensitive to visual cues but potentially less attuned to news sentiment or market tone. An auditorily oriented trader might be more influenced by financial commentary, economic announcements, or the "rhythm" of market activity. A kinesthetic trader, on the other hand, often relies on gut feelings and the physical sensations associated with market moves, such as tension or calmness in the body. Understanding your dominant system allows you to tailor your trading approach, strengthen underused channels, and avoid blind spots that come from relying too heavily on one mode of perception.

Being in Rapport with your own body and mind

I sit and breathe, my thoughts unfold,

A dialogue, both quiet and bold.

Body and mind in gentle accord,

Listening closely, word by word.

No rush, no fight, just steady flow,

The self becomes a friend I know.

One common misconception is the belief that thinking is solely the domain of the rational mind - logical, analytical, and verbal. This view overlooks the profound intelligence embedded in emotion, intuition, and embodied experience. In truth, we think with our whole system: gut instincts, felt senses, dreams, and even relational dynamics all contribute to how we process and respond to the world. The rational mind is a powerful tool, but it's not the only one. Creative insight, moral discernment, and deep decision-making often arise from associative, symbolic, or archetypal sources that defy pure logic. To honor the full spectrum of thinking is to reclaim the wisdom of the body, the heart, and the unconscious.

In NLP, rapport is often discussed in the context of building trust and connection with others, but for traders, the most important relationship is the one they have with their own mind and body. Rapport with yourself means **aligning your conscious intentions with your unconscious patterns**, so your thoughts, emotions, and actions work together rather than against each other. Without this internal alignment, a trader might plan to follow their strategy but find themselves impulsively breaking rules the moment emotions spike. Building rapport with your own mind involves self-awareness, self-compassion, and the ability to communicate internally in a way that fosters trust and cooperation - turning your inner voice into a supportive trading partner rather than a critical saboteur.

Reprogramming Your Internal Dialogue

Recognizing destructive trading self-talk

Destructive trading self-talk often hides in plain sight, quietly eroding confidence and discipline. Phrases like "I always mess this up," "I can't afford another loss," or "I knew I should've..." reinforce fear, hesitation, and self-doubt, making it harder to follow a trading plan. These internal messages can become self-fulfilling prophecies, priming the mind to repeat past mistakes. The first step to breaking the cycle is awareness -

catching these thoughts in real time so they can be challenged, reframed, and replaced with language that supports clear, confident decision-making.

Language patterns that lead to hesitation or revenge trading

The words traders use - both internally and externally -can subtly program their behavior, often leading to hesitation or revenge trading. Phrases like "I'll just wait until it feels right" or "I have to make this money back" shift focus from objective strategy to emotionally charged decision-making. **"Feels right" often masks fear or uncertainty**, causing missed opportunities and over-analysis, while "make it back" frames trading as a battle to recover losses, triggering impulsive, high-risk entries. These language patterns bypass logic, feeding reactive behavior that undermines discipline. By becoming aware of and deliberately reshaping these phrases into process-focused, neutral statements, traders can interrupt the emotional loops that lead to hesitation or revenge trading.

Building an empowering inner dialog and scripts

Empowering inner scripts are intentional, repeatable mental statements that reinforce confidence, discipline, and focus during trading. Instead of letting reactive thoughts like "I can't lose again" or "I have to catch this move" dominate, traders can install proactive scripts such as "I trade my plan, not my emotions" or "My capabilities play out over many trades, not just this one." These scripts act as mental anchors, keeping the mind aligned with long-term process rather than short-term emotional swings. By rehearsing them daily - before markets open, or during moments of indecision, and after trades - traders can recondition their inner dialogue to support calm execution, resilience after losses, and consistent adherence to their strategy. One way we learn is trough repetition and practice. We develop positive as well as negative habits trough practice.

Anchoring in Trading

In an earlier chapter we covered perception limiting anchors in form of fixations – now let's move on to the very useful side of anchoring.

In the volatile world of trading, where sometimes milliseconds matter and emotional turbulence can derail even the most seasoned professional, anchoring offers a quiet, powerful antidote. It's not a strategy in the traditional sense but a psychological tool that stabilizes the inner landscape. Anchoring, in this context, refers to the deliberate use of sensory, symbolic, or ritual cues to evoke a desired mental and emotional state. For traders, that state is often one of clarity, focus, and emotional neutrality - the fertile ground from which disciplined decisions emerge.

The usefulness of anchoring lies in its ability to interrupt reactive patterns and restore coherence. When a trader experiences a loss, a spike in adrenaline, or the creeping fog of doubt, the nervous system shifts into survival mode. Anchors act as gentle reminders - touchstones that say, "You've been here before. You know how to respond." Whether it's a breath pattern, a mantra, a physical gesture, or a visual cue, the anchor becomes a bridge back to the trader's optimal state. It's not magic; it's memory. A memory of flow, of being grounded, of the archetype they've chosen to embody.

Anchoring also reinforces identity. A trader who sees themselves as The Strategist might use a specific token, phrase, or posture to invoke that archetype before entering the market. Over time, this ritual becomes a neural shortcut. The body remembers. The mind follows. Discipline becomes less about resisting impulses and more about returning to a practiced rhythm. Consistency is not enforced - it's invited and self-created.

In high-stakes environments, where uncertainty is constant and control is illusory, anchoring offers a form of internal sovereignty. It allows traders to regulate their emotional state without suppressing it, to engage with risk without being consumed by it. It transforms the trading desk from a battlefield into a place of practice, presence, and precision.

Ultimately, **anchoring is not just useful - it's essential**. It becomes the foundation beneath every resilient trader. The invisible ritual that turns chaos into choreography and performance. And while markets may remain unpredictable, the trader who anchors wisely remains unshaken, moving not from fear or frenzy, but from clarity and choice.

Examples of setting positive Anchors

In volatile environments, discipline and consistency often falter under emotional pressure. When you become able to install and utilize purposeful anchors you can restore:

> ➢ Emotional safety: They signal familiarity and control.
> ➢ Cognitive clarity: Reduce friction and decision fatigue.
> ➢ Identity coherence: Reinforce the archetype you're choosing to embody.
> ➢ Focused Presence: A calm, alert awareness of the market without distraction or mental drift.
> ➢ Emotional Neutrality: Detachment from outcome, free from fear, greed, or regret -ideal for disciplined execution.
> ➢ Strategic Clarity: Confidence in one's plan, with a clear sense of timing, risk, and edge.
> ➢ Resilient Composure: The ability to stay grounded after losses or volatility, without spiraling into reactive behavior.
> ➢ Intuitive Flow: A state where pattern recognition and decision-making feel effortless and embodied.
> ➢ Decisive Action: The readiness to act without hesitation, second-guessing, or paralysis.
> ➢ Curious Observation: Engaging the market with openness and learning mindset, rather than attachment or judgment.
> ➢ Archetypal Embodiment: Stepping into a chosen identity - The Strategist, The Steward, The Alchemist - that guides behavior and emotional posture.

- ➢ Self-Trust: A felt sense of inner authority, where the trader honors their own signals and boundaries.
- ➢ Calibrated Risk Tolerance: A balanced relationship to risk- neither reckless nor avoidant, but intentional and informed.
- ➢ Post-Trade Integration: A reflective state that allows for learning, emotional processing, and ritual closure.

Anchors are especially powerful when paired with archetypal reframing. For example, invoking The Strategist before a trading session, or The Mentor before a coaching call. Installing anchors gives you reliable internal cues that quickly stabilize your state and restore the mindset you want to operate from.

Creating Reference Experiences for Anchoring When None Exist

Anchoring relies on memory. A felt sense. A moment when the body, mind, and spirit aligned in clarity, confidence, or flow. But what happens when a person has no such moment to draw from? No peak performance, no embodied calm, no archetypal resonance to recall?

In my coaching practice I help to create and build reference experiences from the scratch.

This experience doesn't have to be historical - it can be imagined, rehearsed, or ritualized. The nervous system doesn't distinguish between real and vividly envisioned. What it responds to is emotional coherence, sensory detail, and repetition.

Over time, the imagined becomes embodied. The rehearsal becomes memory. The anchor becomes a portal.

This process is not fabrication - it's installation and we model it from someone who can – this becomes a deliberate act of self-authorship. And in high-stakes environments, it's a form of emotional sovereignty. Because when no reference exists, the empowered self creates one.

Creating emotional anchors before market open – Premarket ritual

Creating emotional anchors before the market opens is a powerful way to step into a peak performance state on demand. In NLP, anchoring involves linking a specific physical action - such as pressing two fingers together or taking a deep, deliberate breath- to a desired emotional state like stable confidence, calmness, or focus. Before trading begins, a trader can deliberately recall a time they felt completely in control and successful, intensify that feeling, and set the anchor through their chosen gesture or cue. Repeating this practice daily conditions the mind to associate the action with the resourceful state, allowing the trader to trigger it instantly during live market conditions. This pre-market ritual creates a psychological "launchpad," ensuring decisions are made from a place of clarity and composure rather than stress or hesitation.

Switching Internal state when fear or greed appears

State-switching is the ability to deliberately shift your mental and emotional state the moment you notice fear or greed taking hold. In trading, these emotions can cloud judgment, leading to premature exits, over-leveraged positions, or chasing impulsive setups. NLP provides tools -such as changing your physical posture, altering your breathing rhythm, or triggering a pre-set anchor - that can quickly interrupt the emotional spiral and replace it with a calm, focused state. The key is speed: recognizing the emotional shift **trigger moment** early and switching states before it hijacks your decision-making. By mastering state-switching, traders can neutralize destructive impulses in real time and return to trading from a place of logic and discipline.

The Nature of being in the Zone - Installing "flow state" anchors

My anchor becomes my Lighthouse

Amid the waves, the noise, the night,

I call my inner beacon bright.

Its glow is steady, clear, and true,

A harbor where my calm breaks through.

Touch it once, and I will find,

The strength and calm within my mind.

In high-pressure environments - whether trading, coaching, or leading creative endeavors - achieving a state of flow is often described as the high point of performance. It's that rare and precious moment when time seems to melt away, intuition sharpens, and action unfolds effortlessly. However, flow is not merely a chance occurrence; it is a rhythm that can be cultivated, rehearsed, and invoked through intentional practices.

One of the most effective ways to access this state consistently is through what are called "flow state" anchors. These anchors are deliberate cues - whether physical, sensory, symbolic, or ritualistic - that signal to your nervous system that it is safe to relax into focus and presence. Rather than forcing the flow state, these anchors create a welcoming environment for it to emerge naturally, fostering coherence between mind, body, and spirit.

Flow state anchors might manifest as a specific physical gesture, a certain scent or sound, a meaningful object, or a carefully designed pre-performance ritual. By repeatedly pairing one of these cues with the experience of flow, the brain learns to associate the anchor with the desired state, forming a neuro-emotional shortcut that eases access to peak focus and creativity.

In coaching and trading, where emotional regulation and clear perception are vital, these anchors serve a crucial role. **They cultivate emotional safety by signaling familiarity and control**, reduce cognitive overload by streamlining transitions into high-focus modes, and strengthen the psychological alignment with the role or archetype a person intends to embody - whether that be The Strategist in a trading session or The Mentor during client engagements.

For instance, a simple breathing exercise can act as a powerful anchor, calming the nervous system and centering attention before high-stakes decisions. Physical tokens - like a smooth stone or symbolic coin - can be held or touched to reinforce a sense of identity and purpose. Music or specific soundtracks tied to past peak experiences evoke emotional memories that prepare the mind for flow. Affirming mantras replace fragmented or reactive self-talk with intentional narratives that prime confidence and clarity. Sensory cues such as a distinct scent or a familiar texture ground attention and create a ritualistic transition into work.

Establishing these anchors involves first identifying what the target state of flow feels like personally - whether calm, energized, or intensely focused - and recalling previous moments when that state was experienced. Selecting a resonant cue and intentionally pairing it with the flow state through repetition solidifies the connection. Over time, creating a brief, consistent ritual around this cue allows it to become a reliable gateway to peak performance.

Ultimately, flow is not some mysterious gift bestowed by chance, but a memory etched into our nervous system. Anchors serve as the breadcrumbs guiding us back to that place of alignment and presence. When approached with intention and care, these anchors become sacred rituals- micro-portals into the highest versions of ourselves. They invite not just productivity or achievement, but embodiment, presence, and transformation.

Summarizing: Installing "flow state" anchor means conditioning specific cues - like a piece of music, a breathing pattern, or a physical gesture - to instantly evoke the deep focus, calm, and effortless execution associated with peak performance. By repeatedly pairing the cue with moments of high-quality trading or intense concentration in practice, the brain learns to associate the trigger with that optimal state. Over time, this allows traders to step into flow on demand, bypassing distractions and emotional noise when it matters most. Future pace them before applying, i.e. put yourself in a future position and test the anchor you have set.

Meta-Model & Milton Model in Trading

Let's call it risk management in the domain of our language. In the world of trading, precision is everything - yet the greatest distortions often arise not from market data, but from the trader's own internal language. Milton Erickson's meta model, originally developed within the field of therapeutic hypnosis and later refined in NLP, offers a powerful lens for understanding and disrupting the unconscious patterns that shape decision-making. At its core, the meta model is a tool for clarifying language, challenging assumptions, and restoring access to choice. In trading, where every decision is a reflection of internal state, this becomes not just relevant - but essential.

Traders operate in a landscape of rapid interpretation. They scan charts, headlines, and price action, but they also scan their own thoughts - often without realizing it. Phrases like "I always miss the breakout," "This setup looks dangerous," or "I need to make up for that loss" are not neutral observations. They are linguistic distortions - generalizations, deletions, and distortions - that shape emotional response and behavior. The meta model invites the trader to interrogate these statements. What specifically do you mean by "always"? What makes this setup "dangerous"? According to whom? By asking precise questions, the trader begins to unpack the hidden beliefs and emotional triggers embedded in their self-talk.

This process is not merely cognitive – it gives you direction.

By challenging vague or emotionally loaded language, the trader reduces reactivity and restores clarity. The meta model becomes a form of an internal risk management tool, catching the cognitive biases before they cascade into impulsive action. It also supports the cultivation of discipline, as traders learn to speak to themselves in ways that are specific, grounded, and actionable.

Equally powerful are the presuppositions that underpin the meta model. These are the foundational beliefs that shape how we interpret experience. Presuppositions like "**Every behavior has a positive intention**", "**People make the best choices available to them**" or "**The map is not the territory**" offer a framework for emotional resilience and strategic flexibility. When a trader internalizes the idea that mistakes are feedback, not failure, they become less likely to spiral after a loss. When they accept that their perception of the market is a map - not the market itself - they become more open to adaptation and less attached to being right.

These presuppositions also support the development of archetypal identity. A trader who embodies The Strategist might presuppose that clarity emerges through structure.

One who channels - The Alchemist might presuppose that intuition is a form of pattern recognition. These beliefs shape not just behavior, but emotional posture. They create a container for flow, discipline, and self-trust.

Ultimately, the relevance of the meta model and its presuppositions to trading lies in their ability to restore organization. They help the trader move from reaction to reflection, from linguistic fog to precision, from unconscious bias to intentional choice. In a domain where every tick invites interpretation, and every interpretation invites emotion, the ability to interrogate language becomes a superpower. Not just for performance - but for presence. Not just for profit - but for psychological sovereignty.

Using precise questioning to debug your trading plan

While the Milton Model in NLP is often used to influence others through artfully vague language, traders can reverse its logic by applying *precise questioning* to debug their own trading plans.

This means challenging assumptions, clarifying vague rules, and uncovering hidden gaps in strategy. Questions like "Exactly what market condition triggers this setup?", "How will I know when this trade is no longer valid?", or "What specific data supports this rule?" force the trader to replace ambiguity with clarity. By stripping away fuzzy language and replacing it with measurable, actionable criteria, traders ensure their plan can be executed consistently - even under stress - while reducing the risk of subjective, emotion-driven decisions.

Loosening rigid thinking to adapt to market changes

Rigid thinking can be a trader's downfall, especially in markets that shift character without warning. Clinging to a fixed outlook - such as "this market has to bounce here" or "my strategy always works in this setup" - can blind traders to evolving conditions and lead to mounting losses. NLP techniques like reframing, changing perspectives, and exploring multiple "what if" scenarios help loosen this mental rigidity. By training the mind to consider alternative interpretations of price action and to view market changes as opportunities rather than threats, traders develop the flexibility to adjust position size, timing, or strategy in real time. This adaptability not only preserves capital but also turns unexpected shifts into profitable openings.

Managing Expectations

Expectations serve as a powerful driving force that propel us toward our goals. When set thoughtfully, they create a clear vision of success that fuels persistence and effort. Positive expectations can enhance focus, boost confidence, and inspire continuous improvement. However, the key lies in balancing ambition with realism to maintain motivation without fostering discouragement.

On the other side of the equation, expectations often operate as an unconscious strategy for disappointment: we project how things should unfold, how others should behave, or how we should perform - and then judge reality against that imagined script. The tighter the expectation, the smaller the margin becomes for life to simply be what it is. When reality doesn't match our internal blueprint, frustration, resentment, or self-criticism rush in, not because something truly went wrong, but because our mind was attached to a predetermined outcome. In this way, expectations quietly set the stage for disappointment long before the event ever occurs.

Expectation Audit

Conducting an "Expectations Audit" is a powerful way to bring clarity, alignment, and psychological ease into any project, relationship, or performance context. It involves openly surfacing what each person assumes, hopes for, requires, or fears - before those expectations silently shape behavior. By turning the unspoken into something clearly stated and articulating what was previously assumed, you reduce friction, prevent misunderstandings, and create a shared map of what "success" looks like. An "Expectations Audit" also invites participants to distinguish between realistic commitments, hopeful preferences, and limiting assumptions, allowing for cleaner agreements and more grounded decision-making.

A deeper layer of working with expectations is learning to examine the source of your confidence. Ask yourself, "Is my belief in this outcome and the expectations attached to it grounded in evidence, preparation, and repeated behaviors, or is it merely wishful thinking dressed up as certainty?" This simple inquiry cuts through emotional fog and reveals whether your expectations are calibrated or inflated. It sharpens true confidence because it forces you to reconnect with actual competence, data, and readiness. At the same time, it protects you from slipping into overconfidence - where imagined success replaces real preparation, and the gap between fantasy and reality becomes the breeding ground for disappointment.

Intuition

Whisper of the Mind

A quiet pulse beneath the noise,

A subtle guide, a gentle voice.

It speaks in shapes the eyes can't see,

A truth that moves invisibly.

No logic bends its secret light,

Yet follow it, and paths grow bright.

In a world obsessed with data, metrics, and rational proof, intuition often gets dismissed as narrative enchantment or unreliable gut feeling. But practical intuition - the kind that quietly guides traders, coaches, creatives, and leaders is a cultivated inner compass, forged through experience, emotional attunement, and pattern recognition. That does not mean there is absence of logic, but it is much more a partner, picking up and sensing the field energy.

Practical intuition is the ability to make accurate, timely decisions without conscious reasoning.

Now we are moving into the space of embodied experience where our physical sensations, posture, breath, and movement provide the foundation for intuition because the body continuously processes subtle cues from the environment and internal states. When we "trust our gut," we're really tuning into this embodied wisdom, where lived, sensory experience informs rapid, non-verbal knowing. This way, intuition is grounded through years of exposure to patterns, outcomes, and emotional cues. It is the body's direct engagement with the world.

- ➤ Somatic awareness: The body's subtle signals - tightness, ease, warmth, or contraction.
- ➤ Emotional clarity: Recognizing when fear, hope, or bias is coloring perception.
- ➤ Contextual fluency: Understanding the terrain - whether it's a market, a relationship, or a team dynamic.

How do we learn to pay attention to these subtle clues and how is it cultivated?

Practical intuition is a skill. And like any skill, it can be acquired through deliberate practice.

Your ability to being intuitive depends on several factors.

When intuition is quiet, it doesn't mean it's absent. More often, it's drowned and cluttered out by noise, tension, or unresolved conflict. In states of flight or freeze, the body is not listening for subtle truth; it's scanning for threat. Intuition, which speaks quietly, cannot compete with the noises of survival.

In a flight state, the mind races ahead, trying to escape discomfort. Decisions become reactive, urgent, compulsive. You might mistake speed for clarity or confuse movement with progress. The intuitive signal - often slow, spacious, and nuanced - is bypassed entirely. You're not asking, "What feels true?" How does this fit me? "Am I aligned?" You're asking, "What gets me out of this situation fastest?"

When in a freeze state, the system shuts down. The body goes numb, the mind fogs, and emotional signals flatten. Intuition, which relies on somatic resonance and emotional texture, has no medium to travel through. It's like trying to hear music underwater. You may feel stuck, indecisive, or disconnected - not because you lack insight, but because your inner instruments are muted.

In high-stakes environments, speed is seductive. But intuition thrives in micropauses. Before making a decision, ask:

- ➤ What am I sensing beyond the obvious?
- ➤ Is there a subtle "yes" or "no" in my body?
- ➤ What archetype is active in me right now - The Strategist, The Orphan, The Visionary?

Track Your Hits and Misses

Keep a decision journal. Note when you followed your intuition and what happened. Over time, you'll notice:

Write down what comes up for you – sudden clues – physical sensations – images.

Allow your body to speak to you and not have your rational mind dictating the course of action alone.

Part V – NLP in Action: Trade Execution & Review

Pre-Market Mental Conditioning

Visualization scripts for setups and risk-taking discipline

Visualization scripts allow traders to mentally rehearse both their ideal trade setups and the discipline required to manage risk before a single order is placed. By closing your eyes and vividly picturing a textbook setup forming on the chart - the entry trigger, position sizing, stop placement, and profit target - you prime the brain to recognize and act on it in real time. Just as importantly, the script includes imagining **potential challenges**: price moving against the position, emotions rising, and the trader calmly following their stop-loss plan without hesitation. This mental conditioning strengthens neural pathways for disciplined execution, making it easier to act with precision and confidence when real money is on the line.

Morning routines for cognitive sharpness

A well-designed morning routine primes the mind and body for peak performance before the first trade of the day. Activities such as light exercise, hydration, and mindful breathing increase blood flow and oxygen to the brain, sharpening focus and decision-making ability. Reviewing key market levels, planned setups, and news events activates pattern recognition, while short visualization or anchoring exercises prepare emotional stability. By avoiding distractions - such as doom and worst-case scenarios on social media or reacting to random opinions - traders preserve mental clarity for the sessions ahead. Over time, a consistent morning routine becomes a ritual that signals to the brain: it's time to perform with discipline, precision, and confidence.

In-Trade State Management

Pattern interrupts when panic hits

Pattern interrupts are rapid interventions that break the chain of escalating fear before it derails a trader's decision-making. When panic strikes - often triggered by a sudden market move or an unrealized loss - the mind tends to spiral into worst-case scenarios, leading to impulsive exits or revenge trading. A pattern interrupt can be as simple as standing up and taking three deep, deliberate breaths, splashing cold water on your face, or using a pre-set physical anchor. The goal is to get the nervous system out of the fear loop long enough to regain rational thought. Once the emotional momentum is broken, traders can re-engage their strategy with a calmer, more objective mindset, preventing small setbacks from snowballing into major losses.

Self-hypnosis micro-breaks during market hours

Don't be surprised that I mention Self-hypnosis. We all experience gentle trance states more often than we realize. For some people the word hypnosis creates uneasiness about losing or not being in control. But keep in mind in this case it's self-induced and you are allowing the flow.

When you listen to someone's lecture you find interesting and stimulating, you will not notice the passage of time. But if the lecture is boring you may be aware of the hardiness of the chair or the heat in the room.

We are all familiar with "Day Dreaming".

When driving on autopilot you sometimes realize how far you have already gone without noticing it, or perhaps you even missed your exit.

When listen to certain music – you can get lost in memories and emotions – and music can be a powerful auditory anchor – putting you back in time and eliciting emotions you have associated with a certain experience.

Watching flames in the fireplace or getting lost observing ripples on the water.

Now let's define for our purpose self-hypnosis as taking micro-breaks, intentional mental resets that help traders maintain focus and emotional balance during long trading sessions. By closing the eyes, slowing the breath, and using a simple mental script - such as visualizing a calm, steady body of water or repeating a relaxation cue - a trader can quickly lower stress levels and clear mental clutter. You can be creative and find what fit's and works for you. These breaks, lasting just one to three minutes, allow the nervous system to shift from high alert back to a state of relaxed awareness, reducing the likelihood of impulsive decisions. When practiced regularly, self-hypnosis micro-breaks become a powerful tool for sustaining concentration, managing fatigue, and keeping emotional states in check while the markets are moving. We can even fuse them with certain anchors for confidence.

Post-Trade Debrief with NLP

The "Trading Feedback Loop" model

In the world of trading, performance is not just about execution - it's about reflection. The "Trading Feedback Loop" model offers a dynamic framework for cultivating discipline, emotional regulation, and strategic refinement through continuous self-awareness. Rather than treating each trade as an isolated event, this model views trading as a cyclical process of action, observation, interpretation, and adjustment. It transforms the trader from a reactive participant into a reflective practitioner.

At the heart of the feedback loop is the recognition that every trade - win or loss - is data. Not just market data, but psychological data as well. How did the trader feel before entering the position? What internal narratives were active? Was the decision driven by clarity or compulsion? These questions form the first layer of the loop: post-trade reflection. It's not enough to log the outcome; the trader must log the state of mind, the emotional attitude, and the archetype they were embodying at the time. This creates a rich archive of experiential insight that can be revisited and decoded.

The second layer is pattern recognition. Over time, the trader begins to notice recurring themes - certain biases that emerge under pressure, certain setups that trigger overconfidence, certain emotional states that precede poor decisions. These patterns are gold. They reveal the trader's unique psychological fingerprint and offer a roadmap for disruption and recalibration. The feedback loop becomes a mirror, showing not just what happened, but why it happened.

The third layer is ritualized adjustment. Once patterns are identified, the trader can design micro-interventions - anchoring rituals, reframed mantras, environmental cues - that support realignment. For example, if a trader notices that impulsive entries often follow a loss, they might install a post-loss ritual: a breath cycle, a mantra, a pause. This doesn't just prevent reactive behavior - it reinforces emotional sovereignty. The feedback loop becomes a training ground for identity, where the trader chooses who they want to be in the face of volatility.

Importantly, the loop is not linear - it's recursive. Each cycle deepens awareness, sharpens discipline, and expands the trader's capacity for flow. It's a living system, adaptable to changing market conditions and evolving personal goals. And it's not just for individuals. Teams and firms can adopt the model to foster a culture of reflection, psychological safety, and continuous improvement.

Ultimately, the Trading Feedback Loop is a model of integration. It weaves together action and awareness, performance and presence, strategy and soul. It invites the trader to move beyond outcome obsession and into a deeper relationship with process. Because in trading, as in life, mastery is not found in perfection - it's found in the willingness to learn, adjust, and return. Again, and again.

The "Trading Feedback Loop" model frames every trade as both a performance and a learning opportunity. It begins with executing a trade based on a clearly defined plan, followed by an immediate, objective review of the outcome - not just in terms of profit or loss, but in how closely the execution matched the intended process. This is then followed by extracting specific lessons, such as refining entry timing, adjusting risk management, or improving emotional control. These insights are incorporated back into the trading plan and mindset preparation, ensuring that each trade, win or lose, strengthens future performance. By treating trading as an iterative cycle rather than a series of isolated events, the feedback loop transforms mistakes into assets and accelerates skill development over time.

Reframing losses to accelerate skill acquisition

Reframing losses is the practice of viewing losing trades not as failures, but as tuition payments for skill development. Instead of dwelling on the emotional sting or the monetary setback, traders consciously extract the lesson hidden within - whether it's a flaw in analysis, a lapse in discipline, or a market condition they hadn't fully accounted for. This shift in perspective turns losses into actionable data points, reducing the shame and frustration that can sabotage future performance. By normalizing losses as part of the growth process, traders maintain curiosity, resilience, and motivation, enabling them to adapt faster and compound their skill set over time.

Part VI – Advanced Applications

Modeling Top Traders

The NLP modeling process involves identifying and replicating the mental strategies, belief systems, and behavioral patterns of elite traders to accelerate one's own growth. Rather than simply copying their trade setups, modeling digs deeper into how top performers perceive market information, manage internal state under pressure, and make rapid yet disciplined decisions. This includes studying their language patterns, internal representations, risk frameworks, and recovery routines after setbacks. By breaking these elements into teachable and repeatable components, a trader can integrate the core success factors of high achievers into their own practice, effectively compressing years of trial-and-error learning into a shorter, more focused developmental path.

Reverse-engineering decision patterns, not just strategies

Reverse-engineering decision patterns means looking beyond the surface of a trader's strategy to uncover *how* and *why* they make specific choices under different market conditions. While strategies outline the "what" of trading - entries, exits, and risk parameters - decision patterns reveal the mental sequencing, prioritization of information, and emotional calibration that drive those strategies in real time. By analyzing thought processes, triggers for action, and criteria for standing aside, traders can identify the underlying cognitive architecture that leads to consistent performance. This deeper level of understanding allows them to adapt principles to new market environments, rather than rigidly following a system that may eventually become obsolete.

Timeline Work for Trading Upsets

Sometimes we need to "Rewire the Past to Reclaim the Present" - TW aims to dissolve emotional patterns and limiting beliefs at their origin. Rather than focusing on the specifics of past events, it explores how those experiences are encoded in the mind's internal timeline, where they are stored and how their emotional charge persists into current behavior.

Clearing emotional baggage from big losses

Big losses can leave a psychological residue that silently influences future trading decisions, leading to hesitation, overprotection, or revenge trading. Clearing this emotional baggage it's not just simply done by "moving on" - we want to deliberately process the event to separate the factual lessons from the emotional charge. In NLP we use techniques such as timeline work, submodality shifts, and reframing that can help traders rewire the memory, so it no longer triggers fear or self-doubt. In my early NLP days (1983) we utilized a method called "Change History". The process involved dissociating the client from the initial memory as they moved back along their timeline, with careful attention to the trigger elements that produced the undesired emotional state. Once anchored in a resourceful and fully dissociated state, the client viewed and replayed the event from a second- or third-position vantage point. Submodality shifts were then applied to restructure the experience while preventing any re-traumatization.

One fundamental question arose in this context "what kind of personal qualities and resources would I have needed at that time to deal effectively with this situation?" With these qualities now fully installed, we can direct our client to transport these internal resources back to the original memory, integrate them and voila' you construct a different reference experience for this event.

Since then, a great deal of research has been done how we store memories of past events. Are these memories arranged in a proper internal timeline and held in a part of the brain that keeps them from interfering with our current experience!

By neutralizing this past emotional impact, the trader regains access to their full decision-making capacity, allowing them to re-enter the market with confidence, objectivity, and a forward-focused mindset.

But there's another breakthrough that stands above the rest in its importance – with Timeline Work we are not only rewriting the past, but we can install compelling future outcomes aligned with values, identity, and purpose, making certain that change is not only corrective, but generative. This happens when creating congruence between intention, action, habits and long-term direction.

Ultimately, Timeline Work does not erase the past. The purpose is to get you into the driver seat, to honor the emotional truth of trading trauma or upset while refusing to let that moment define the future. In high-stakes environments, where psychological resilience is as critical as technical skill, this kind of inner work becomes foundational - not just for performance, but for identity.

When a trader heals the timeline, they don't just change how they trade - they change how they relate to risk, to uncertainty, and to themselves. The market becomes less of a battlefield and more a space for self-realization shaping trader identity. Each session becomes an opportunity to practice presence, to reinforce sovereignty, and to embody the archetype they've chosen to lead with.

Because every trader carries a timeline. And within that timelines are moments waiting to be rewritten - not with denial, but with dignity, learning and with full integration. And when those moments are healed, the trader doesn't just perform better - they become whole. In this moment your future is no longer determined by a sometimes-single incident. Your history will change in retrospect if the timeline is healed.

Releasing Fear of Pulling the Trigger

Many traders know the frustration of spotting a setup, watching the market align perfectly with their plan, and yet freezing at the moment of execution. The fear of pulling the trigger is one of the most common and costly psychological barriers in trading. It often stems from a combination of past losses, perfectionism, and the subconscious belief that a single trade can make or break one's future. This hesitation not only causes missed opportunities but also erodes confidence over time, creating a self-reinforcing loop of doubt and inaction.

The first step in overcoming this fear is to understand its root causes. For some, it's a memory of a large, painful loss that remains emotionally "charged." For others, it's the need for certainty in an inherently uncertain environment. NLP offers practical tools for dissolving these blocks by changing the way the brain encodes risk and opportunity. Techniques such as submodality shifts can alter the intensity of past loss memories, while anchoring can help install states of calm focus before trade execution.

Another powerful approach is to redefine what "success" means in the moment. Instead of attaching success to the outcome of the trade, attach it to following your process flawlessly. This reframing removes the pressure to be right and shifts the focus to what is actually controllable - execution quality and risk management. When traders consistently reward themselves for executing their plan, regardless of outcome, fear gives way to trust in the process.

Practical drills can also help desensitize the trigger moment. For example, simulated trading sessions that focus solely on rapid decision-making can build execution muscle memory without the emotional load of real capital. Combining these with short visualization scripts - mentally rehearsing perfect execution - creates a bridge between intention and action in the heat of the moment.

Ultimately, releasing the fear of pulling the trigger is about transforming the internal narrative from *"What if I'm wrong?"* to *"I am prepared, and I execute."* Once a trader decouples self-worth from individual trade outcomes and aligns emotionally with their strategy, pulling the trigger becomes a natural, confident action rather than a nerve-wracking leap into the unknown.

Self-Calibration & Sensory Acuity

Reading your own micro-signals of hesitation or reactivity

In trading, the body often whispers warnings before the mind consciously recognizes them. Micro-signals - such as a quickened heartbeat, shallow breathing, tightened jaw, or an urge to click without reviewing your plan- are subtle cues that hesitation or impulsivity is taking over. By training yourself to notice these shifts in posture, breathing, or internal dialogue, you gain a crucial early-warning system. NLP's emphasis on sensory acuity allows traders to map these micro-responses and link them to specific mental states, enabling a quick pause, a deep breath, or a mental reset before acting. Over time, reading these signals becomes a form of self-surveillance that prevents emotional sabotage and maintains disciplined execution.

Improving situational awareness for market conditions

Improving situational awareness in trading means developing the ability to read the market's "mood" in real time and adapt accordingly. It's more than watching price charts - it involves noticing the interplay between volatility, volume, news flow, and the behavior of correlated markets. NLP techniques can sharpen this awareness by training traders to calibrate both external cues (such as sudden shifts in order flow) and internal states (such as overconfidence or doubt creeping in). By continually scanning for context - asking, *"What kind of market am I in right now?"* Traders can match their strategy to prevailing conditions, avoiding the trap of applying yesterday's tactics to today's environment. This heightened perception becomes a competitive advantage, turning raw market data into meaningful, actionable insight.

Part VII – The Road to Trading Mastery

Integrating NLP into a Trading Journal

Language pattern tracking in trade notes

Language pattern tracking in trade notes involves reviewing not just the technical details of a trade, but the exact words and phrases you use to describe your thinking before, during, and after execution. The language you choose often reveals unconscious beliefs, emotional states, and decision biases - such as "I had to take the trade" (pressure-driven) or "I didn't want to miss out" (FOMO-driven). By systematically recording and analyzing these patterns, traders can detect recurring mental traps, hesitation triggers, or overconfidence cues. NLP treats language as a mirror reflecting cognitive processes and makes this practice especially powerful. In this process you can rewrite unhelpful patterns into clearer, more empowering self-talk that supports disciplined, process-driven performance.

Rating trades by emotional state as well as P/L

Rating trades by emotional state as well as P/L adds a deeper dimension to performance analysis, revealing patterns that pure numbers can't capture. A profitable trade taken in a state of panic may signal poor process despite a positive outcome, while a small loss executed with calm discipline could indicate strong decision-making. By tagging trades with emotional ratings - such as calm, anxious, overconfident, or hesitant - traders can spot correlations between specific states and long-term profitability. This NLP-informed approach trains awareness of the internal conditions that consistently support high-quality execution, making it easier to replicate them and reduce the influence of unhelpful states on future trades.

Designing Your "Trader's Operating System

Combining strategy, state management, and reflection

Combining strategy, managing your internal state, and reflection creates a holistic framework for consistent trading performance. A sound strategy provides the technical edge, internal state management ensures you can execute it without emotional interference, and reflection turns each trade into a learning opportunity. When these elements work together, traders don't just react to markets - they respond with precision, self-awareness, and adaptability. NLP tools enhance this integration by aligning mental states with strategic intent and using structured post-trade reviews to refine both execution and mindset. The result is a feedback loop where skill, psychology, and self-knowledge reinforce one another, steadily raising the trader's competence and confidence.

Creating a repeatable process for growth

Creating a repeatable process for growth in trading means building a structured cycle that can be executed and refined over time - regardless of market conditions. This involves clearly defining your setup criteria, risk parameters, and execution rules, then pairing them with consistent state management techniques to maintain focus and emotional balance. Reflection and journaling become the mechanisms for feedback, helping you identify what's working, what needs adjustment, and how to implement those changes without disrupting your core process. By treating growth as a deliberate, methodical routine rather than a byproduct of random wins, traders embed discipline, adaptability, and continuous improvement into their practice, making progress measurable and sustainable.

Mantras

Mantras are short, repeated phrases or affirmations which can become surprisingly powerful tools.

A trading mantra helps a trader stay grounded, focused, and emotionally balanced. By repeating a phrase such as "Trade the plan, not the emotions" or "Patience pays", a trader reinforces discipline and consistency. In moments of stress or excitement - after a losing streak or before a big move -such reminders can interrupt impulsive behavior and bring the trader back to a rational mindset.

Mantras also serve as anchors for mental clarity. Regular repetition creates a form of mental conditioning, training the brain to associate certain words with calmness and confidence. This is especially useful in volatile markets, where quick decisions can easily be swayed by fear or greed.

Furthermore, mantras encourage self-awareness. By consciously using affirmations that reflect core trading principles - such as risk management, patience, or humility - traders build stronger emotional resilience. Over time, this can lead to improved consistency, reduced stress, and better decision-making.

In essence, mantras are practical mental frameworks helping also form and shape a traders identity. Just as traders use charts to interpret the market, mantras help interpret and regulate one's inner landscape. When mind and method align, trading becomes not only more effective, but also more sustainable.

The Self-Evolving Trader

Continuous NLP practice

Continuous NLP practice in trading is about embedding mental conditioning into your daily routine so that psychological resilience and peak performance become second nature. Just as strategies require regular review and testing, NLP techniques - such as anchoring resourceful states, reframing setbacks, and refining self-talk - need consistent application to remain effective under pressure. This means rehearsing mental scripts before market open, using state-switching tools during live trading, and reflecting afterward to reinforce learning. Over time, practice and repetition hardwires constructive thought patterns and emotional responses, allowing traders to adapt fluidly to market changes without being derailed by stress or impulsiveness. In this way, NLP becomes not a tool you occasionally use, but a constant part of how you trade.

You think you have reached the summit

Avoiding plateaus in skill development requires deliberately pushing beyond comfort zones while maintaining a structured growth process. Nothing grows in the comfort zone. In trading, this means regularly reviewing performance data, identifying areas of stagnation, and introducing targeted challenges - such as experimenting with new market conditions, refining risk management tactics, or testing variations of proven setups.

NLP techniques can help break through mental barriers by uncovering limiting beliefs, reprogramming unhelpful patterns, and keeping motivation aligned with deeper values. By combining strategic experimentation with psychological agility, traders transform plateaus into springboards, ensuring their skills evolve in pace with the ever-changing markets rather than settling into complacency.

Reflections on trading as a lifelong game of mastery

Trading, at its core, is a lifelong game of mastery - an evolving interplay between skill, psychology, and self-awareness. Markets will never stop changing, and neither will the challenges they present, which means the true pursuit isn't a final victory, but the continuous sharpening of perception, discipline, and adaptability. Mastery in trading is less about "arriving" and more about cultivating a mindset that thrives on learning, embraces uncertainty, and uses every win and loss as fuel for growth. NLP adds a powerful dimension to this journey by giving traders tools to manage state, refine thinking, and align identity with their expertise. Trading becomes more than a career or a source of income - it becomes a personal evolution, measured not only in profits, but in the depth of skill and the quality thinking and state of the mind behind each decision.

Coaching & Self-Work Process

In trading, the most volatile asset is the mind behind the screen. Coaching and self-work in this domain go far beyond strategy optimization; they're about cultivating the trader's internal architecture. This process begins with awareness:

noticing patterns of fear, overconfidence, avoidance, or compulsive action. Through guided reflection, journaling, and archetypal mapping, traders learn to decode their emotional signals as important data.

Coaching introduces meta-decisions: higher-order choices that shape how tactical decisions are made. (Decisions about how to make decisions). These include setting emotional safety protocols, designing rituals for bias disruption, and choosing which criteria govern entry, exit, and pause. Self-work deepens this by exploring identity - who the trader becomes under pressure, in loss, or in gain. The goal isn't just performance; it's coherence. When the trader's values, habits, and decision-making protocols align, the market becomes a mirror, not a battlefield.

Ultimately, coaching in trading is not about controlling outcomes - it's about transforming the one who trades. The charts may reflect price, but the process reveals character.

Most important character traits successful traders

Step 1: Awareness

Keep a trading journal noting moments when your actions differ from your plan.

Mark emotions and thoughts in the moment e.g. "fear of missing out", "justifying decision".

Step 2: Identify - the Belief Conflict

Identifying the belief conflict means surfacing the emotional logic beneath the behavior.

Ask: What belief is being challenged right now?

Examples: "I'm a disciplined trader vs. "I can't close this losing position."

"I must be in control to succeed vs. markets are unpredictable and can't be controlled."

"I need to prove my competence by being right vs. Good traders admit when they're wrong and cut losses quickly."

"Trading gives me freedom to do what I want vs. Consistency requires strict rules and routines".

Step 3: Reframe

Replace ego-protective thoughts with performance-oriented thinking.

Example: "Closing this loss is evidence of my discipline, not a sign of weakness."

Step 4: Align Systems with Psychology

Use rules that prevent dissonance triggers:

Automated stops.

Pre-commitment contracts ("If X happens, I will Y").

Risk defined before entry.

Most important character traits successful traders possess

1. Discipline in Execution, Risk Management, Psychological and Emotional, Strategy, Time and Routine

In modeling, disciplined traders show consistent adherence to setups, risk parameters, and position sizing.

2. Patience

Waiting for high-probability setups instead of forcing trades.

Modeled behavior: top traders often spend far more time observing than executing, entering only when the edge is clear.

3. Emotional Regulation

Keeping fear and greed in check, especially during volatile market swings.

Stay in their optimal mental state regardless of recent wins or losses.

4. Adaptability

Adjusting strategies when market conditions change without clinging to outdated methods.

Have mental flexibility to evolve with volatility, trends, and macro shifts.

5. Risk Awareness

Seeing preservation of capital as the first priority.

Think in probabilities, manage drawdowns, and never let a single loss threaten the career.

6. Resilience

Recovering quickly from losses, mistakes, or drawdowns without losing confidence.

Treat setbacks as data, not personal failures.

7. Decisiveness

Acting quickly and confidently when a valid opportunity presents itself.

In modeling, don't get stuck in analysis paralysis - decision-making speed matches market pace.

The difference between impulsive and decisive lies in the source of action and the quality of awareness behind it – reactive vs. responsive.

Impulsivity is speed without clarity; decisiveness is clarity in motion.

8. Curiosity & Continuous Learning

Studying markets, strategies, and self-improvement methods.

Treat trading as a lifelong apprenticeship, never assuming they've "figured it out."

9. Self-Awareness

Understanding personal strengths, weaknesses, biases, and emotional triggers.

Actively monitor their mental state to avoid destructive impulses.

10. Focus on Process Over Outcome

Measuring success by following the plan rather than by the result of a single trade.

Know that consistent execution leads to consistent returns over time.

The Ultimate Traders Mindset - Complete NLP Toolkit

(Quick reference for daily use)

1. Mindset Reprogramming

- ➤ **The "Market-as-Teacher" Frame** – Start your day with: *"The market is my coach, not my enemy."*
- ➤ **Future Self Calibration** – Imagine meeting your top trading self in 5 years; ask what they mastered first.
- ➤ **Belief Change** – Replace "I'm unlucky" with *"I'm refining my edge every day."*
- ➤ **Three-Win Recall** – Mentally replay three moments of perfect discipline before the first trade.
- ➤ **Identity Statement** – Affirm: *"I am a trader who learns faster than I fail."*
- ➤ **Purpose Anchor** – Keep a visible reminder of *why* you trade where you can see it during market hours.

> ➢ **Micro-Victory Recognition** – Celebrate flawless execution even on losing trades.

2. Managing Internals States

Physiology Reset – Use 4-7-8 breathing to drop tension before pulling the trigger.

Anchor Confidence – Associate a touch gesture with a memory of your best trade.

Micro Break Hypnosis – 90-second mental reset: breathe + mantra + visual calm scene.

Panic Pattern Interrupt – Stand up, shake, spin 180° look in the sky and take a deep breath, and re-look at the chart.

Pre-Market Power Posture – Embodying Clarity before the Chaos

The Pre-Market Power Posture is a somatic ritual designed to align body, breath, and intention before engaging with the market. It's not just a stance - it's a signal to the nervous system: I am grounded, aware, and ready. By adopting an upright, open posture - feet planted, spine tall, shoulders relaxed - the trader interrupts slouching patterns of doubt or urgency. When paired with breathwork (like 4-7-8) and a spoken meta-decision e.g. "I trade from clarity, not compulsion", this posture becomes a physical anchor for emotional safety and strategic focus.

In volatile environments, posture is often the first thing to collapse. Reclaiming it before the bell rings is a way to embody your hierarchy of criteria - placing presence, discipline, and coherence above reactive gain. It's a ritual of readiness, a stance of sovereignty.

Greed Switch-Off – Resetting your Inner Appetit

is a conscious ritual designed to interrupt the emotional surge of overreach - the moment when a trader begins chasing profit beyond reason, clarity, or alignment. Greed often masquerades as momentum, but beneath it lies fear of missing out, identity inflation, or unresolved scarcity. This switch-off is not about suppressing ambition; it's about restoring coherence.

Practically, it may involve stepping away from the screen, engaging in a breathwork cycle (like 4-7-8), or revisiting a pre-written meta-decision: "I trade to express discipline, not to prove worth." Symbolically, it's a circuit breaker -a way to re-anchor in values, reframe the moment, and re-enter the market with integrity.

When integrated into a trader's hierarchy of criteria, the Greed Switch-Off becomes a sacred pause: a brief silence that protects long-term mastery from short-term noise.

When feeling euphoric, deliberately walk away for 2 minutes before re-checking positions.

From Fear to Focus

The Fear-to-Focus Drill is a rapid emotional recalibration technique that transforms reactive fear into grounded clarity.

It's built for moments when the nervous system spikes - after a sudden market move, a looming loss, or anticipatory dread. Instead of suppressing fear, the drill acknowledges it as signal, then channels it into structured action.

Step 1: **Name the Fear**

Silently or aloud, identify the fear's voice: "I'm afraid of missing out," "I'm afraid of being wrong," etc. Naming disarms the shadow.

Step 2: **Anchor the Body**

Adopt your Pre-Market Power Posture - feet grounded, spine tall. Pair it with one round of 4-7-8 breathing to reset your physiology.

Step 3: **Reframe the Moment**

Use a meta-decision mantra: "I trade to express discipline, not to chase validation." This shifts the frame from threat to intention.

Step 4: **Micro-Action**

Take one small, focused action: review your hierarchy of criteria, check your bias checklist, or journal a single sentence. This restores agency.

The drill takes less than 90 seconds but rewires the emotional circuitry. Over time, it becomes a ritual of resilience - a way to meet fear not with avoidance, but with structured presence.

Label fear out loud, then shift to *"What's the next smallest, smartest action?"*

Cognitive Clarity

> ➤ **Bias Check Question** – "If this setup appeared last week, would I take it?"
> ➤ **Illusion of Control Test** – Remove one tool and assess clarity for the day.

The Illusion of Control Test invites a subtle yet powerful recalibration: remove one familiar tool - be it a journaling prompt, a decision protocol, or a symbolic anchor - and observe how the day unfolds without it. This gentle disruption reveals where clarity arises from genuine awareness versus habitual behavior. By stripping away one layer of perceived control, we expose the raw architecture of our thinking, allowing deeper patterns, biases, or intuitive insights to surface.

> ➤ **Hindsight Detox** – Journal *before* entries to avoid justifying after the fact.
> ➤ **Language Audit** – Swap rigid words ("must," "have to") for flexible ones ("choose," "decide").
> ➤ **Pattern Spotter** – Weekly, identify a recurring thought before bad trades.
> ➤ **Clarity Cue** – Keep a sticky note with *"What is the market showing me, not what I want to see?"*
> ➤ **Multi-Frame View** – Force yourself to check at least 2 different timeframes before entry.

Skill Acceleration

➤ **Two-Minute Visualization** – Imagine spotting and executing your A+ setup perfectly.

➤ **Feedback Loop Review** – Weekly: 1 strength + 1 improvement target.

➤ **Reverse Model** – Study *thinking patterns* of elite traders, not just setups.

➤ **Loss Reframe Drill** – Turn every loss into a "tuition payment" for a skill.

➤ **10-Trade Challenge** – Trade only your A+ setup for 10 trades in a row; track results.

➤ **Post-Trade Voice Note** – Speak your learning aloud within 2 minutes of closing a position.

➤ **Setup Dissection** – Break your best trade into 5 micro-decisions you can replicate.

Emotional Mastery

➤ **Trigger Journal** – Track what market events spark your strongest emotional responses.

➤ **Delayed Entry Rule** – When emotional, delay execution by at least 3 minutes.

➤ **Loss Reset Ritual** – After a loss, perform a consistent, calming physical ritual before the next trade.

➤ **Gratitude Interrupt** – Think of 3 non-trading things you're grateful for when tilted.

➤ **Hesitation Scan** – Notice breath holding or muscle tension before placing an order.

- ➤ **Greed Diffuser** – Ask: *"If I wasn't already in this trade, would I enter now?"*

NLP Techniques in Action

- ➤ **Submodality Shift** – Make the mental image of a fear smaller, dimmer, and farther away.
- ➤ **Belief Installation** – Visualize patience, resilience, adaptability as glowing symbols you "wear" during trading.
- ➤ **Morning Script** – Recite a brief visualization of spotting setups + executing with discipline.
- ➤ **State Switch Gesture** – Create a physical trigger to move from fear to focus.
- ➤ **Flow Trigger Installation** – Link a sound or gesture to a memory of peak performance.
- ➤ **Milton Debugging** – Use precise, open-ended questions to clarify trade plans.
- ➤ **Shadow Check** – Spot hidden biases in your goals before they sabotage execution.

Reflection & Long-Term Growth

- ➤ **Emotional P/L Rating** – Score each trade for emotional state, not just dollars.
- ➤ **Strategy-State-Reflection Combo** – Journal how your mindset affected your setups.
- ➤ **Growth Process Mapping** – Write down your repeatable improvement cycle.
- ➤ **Continuous NLP Drill** – Practice one NLP skill daily, even if markets are closed.

- ➢ **Plateau Breaker** – Change environment, review old notes, seek outside feedback.
- ➢ **Mastery Mindset Mantra** – *"I'm here for the next decade, not the next trade."*
- ➢ **Quarterly Identity Review** – Check if your "trader persona" is evolving toward your ideal self

Daily NLP Exercises for Traders

1. Pre-Market Pattern Priming

Purpose: Align mind with market clarity before the first trade.
How:

- ➢ Close your eyes, breathe deeply for 1 minute.
- ➢ Imagine scanning the market calmly, spotting your A+ setup.
- ➢ Mentally *step into* your body in that moment - feel your hands on the mouse, see the chart, hear your breath.
- ➢ Anchor the feeling by squeezing thumb and forefinger together.
Duration: 3 minutes.

2. State-to-Strategy Link

Purpose: Match emotional state with optimal trade decisions.
How:

- ➢ Think of your best trading day ever.
- ➢ Notice your breathing, posture, tone of internal voice.
- ➢ While holding that state, visualize executing today's planned setup.

- ➤ Anchor it with a physical gesture (e.g., touching your wrist).
  Duration: 5 minutes.

3. Submodality Reframe for Losses

Purpose: Reduce emotional charge from past bad trades.
How:

- ➤ Bring up the memory of a painful trade.
- ➤ Shrink the image, make it blurry, and move it farther away in your mind.
- ➤ Replace it with a bright, close-up mental movie of a perfect execution.
- ➤ Repeat until the emotional sting fades.
  Duration: 5 minutes.

4. Micro-Signal Awareness Drill

Purpose: Spot hesitation or impulsiveness before acting.
How:

- ➤ Just before placing any order, pause for 5 seconds.
- ➤ Scan: Is my breath shallow? Are my shoulders tense? Is my inner voice rushed?
- ➤ If yes, reset with one slow breath and confirm the setup meets all rules.
  Duration: Ongoing in-session habit.

5. Language Pattern Tracking

Purpose: Reveal subconscious bias in trade notes.
How:

- ➢ After each trade, write one sentence about *why* you entered and exited.
- ➢ End of day, highlight emotionally charged words ("had to," "should," "felt lucky").
- ➢ Replace them with neutral, factual descriptions.
  Duration: 10 minutes post-market.

6. Emotional P/L Scoring

Purpose: Build awareness of state-impact on results.
How:

- ➢ At the end of the day, rate each trade 1–10 for emotional clarity.
- ➢ Compare the emotional score trend to your P/L.
- ➢ Notice where discipline or overtrading patterns emerge.
  Duration: 5 minutes daily review.

7. Identity Reinforcement Visualization

Purpose: Strengthen trader identity at the subconscious level.
How:

- ➢ Imagine yourself 1 year from now, trading with discipline and mastery.
- ➢ See through your own eyes, feel the confidence, hear your inner calm.

> ➢ Bring that identity back into today's market session.
> **Duration:** 3 minutes pre-market.

Changing Internal States

1. Internal State Change Script - From Hesitation to Clarity

Goal: Quickly shift from indecision to focused execution.

Use when: You spot a setup but feel yourself hesitating.

Step 1 - Interrupt:

"Stop. Step back from the screen. Take one deep, slow breath."

Step 2 - Reset physiology:

"Roll your shoulders back, plant your feet, feel the chair supporting you."

Step 3 - Install new state:

"Inhale clarity... exhale doubt. Picture the trade fully formed, as if it has already played out according to plan. Hear your voice say, 'This is my setup. This is my process.'"

Step 4 - Action:

"Move your hand to the mouse only when you feel the calm weight of certainty in your chest."

2. Reframing Script - Turning Losses into Lessons

Goal: Reduce emotional sting from a loss while extracting useful insight.

Use when: Reviewing losing trades post-market.

Step 1 - Shift perspective:

"This trade is feedback on my system and state in that moment - not a verdict on my trading capabilities"

Step 2 - Re-label:

"Instead of calling it a loss, I'll call it tuition. The market is my teacher, and this is part of the curriculum."

Step 3 - Extract the lesson:

"What was the single most useful insight I gained from this trade? Write it down now."

Step 4 - Future-focus:

"Now I see the same setup in the future, and I execute with the improved version of me that learned today's lesson."

3. Anchoring Script - Installing a "Ready to Trade" Trigger

Goal: Create a consistent emotional entry point before trading.

Use when: Pre-market preparation.

Step 1 - Recall peak state:

"Think of your best trading day - when you were calm, confident, and precise. See the charts clearly, feel the mouse in your hand, hear the quiet certainty in your thoughts."

Step 2 - Intensify:

"Turn up the brightness of the image, bring the feeling closer, make it stronger in your chest."

Step 3 - Anchor:

"As that feeling peak, press your thumb and forefinger together or find another physical anchor you feel comfortable with and say silently, 'Ready.'"

Step 4 - Test:

"Break state - look around the room, think of something random - then press thumb and forefinger together. Feel the shift return. That's your trigger."

My advice – Do not overload! This book is comprehensive. Focus on small sections until you are mastering the process and the process becomes second nature. Thereafter you can move on to the next. It does not have to be in a particular order, and you select what's most important to you.

In the end, mastery in trading - and in life - isn't found in control, but in relationship to uncertainty, to emotion and to oneself. Every breath taken before reacting, every moment of awareness amid chaos, becomes a quiet act of self-trust. These micro-moments of safety form the invisible architecture beneath consistency and confidence. The market will always move, but who you are within that movement determines everything. When safety is internal, presence replaces panic -

and trading becomes not a fight for survival, but an expression of clarity, discipline, and flow.

Enjoy the ride and realize the difference it will make for you!

Bibliography

A Gestalt Coaching Primer – Dorothy E. Siminovitch PH.D. MCC

ADHD - A Hunter in a Farmer's World – Thom Hartmann

Atomic Habits – James Clear

Bad Therapy – Abigail Shrier

Changing Belief Systems with NLP – Robert Dilts

From Coach to Awakener – Robert Dilts

Games People Play - Eric Berne, MD

Generative Coaching – Volume 1 – Robert Dilts and Stephen Gilligan

How to Argue and Win Every Time – Gerry Spence

Inner Work - Robert A. Johnson

NLP The Essential Guide – Tom Hoobyar, Tom Dotz, Susan Sanders

On Becoming a Person - Carl Rogers

Owning Your Own Shadow – Robert. A Johnson

Practical Intuition - Laura Day

Precision – A New Approach to Communication – Michael McMaster and John Grinder

Solutions – Leslie Cameron Bandler

Structure of Magic – Volume 1 and 2 – John Grinder and Richard Bandler

The Culture Advantage - Daniel Strode

The Emotional Hostage – Leslie Cameron Bandler, Michael Lebeau

The Emprint Method – Leslie, Cameron-Bandler, David Gordon, Michael Lebeau

The Hidden Connections – Fritjof Capra

The Mental Game of Trading – Jared Tendler, MS

The New People Making – Virgina Satir

The Psychopathology of Every Day Life – Sigmund Freud

The Purpose Factor – Brian Bosche', Gabrielle Bosche"

www.ingramcontent.com/pod-product-compliance
Lightning Source LLC
Chambersburg PA
CBHW072226270326
41930CB00010B/2007